Be Charming: Modern Manners

Be Charming: Modern Manners
Edward Cyster and
Francesca Young

For UK order enquiries: please contact
Bookpoint Ltd, 130 Milton Park, Abingdon, Oxon OX14 4SB.
Telephone: +44 (0) 1235 827720. Fax: +44 (0) 1235 400454.
Lines are open 09.00–17.00, Monday to Saturday, with a 24-hour
message answering service. Details about our titles and how to
order are available at www.teachyourself.com

For USA order enquiries: please contact McGraw-Hill Customer
Services, PO Box 545, Blacklick, OH 43004-0545, USA.
Telephone: 1-800-722-4726. Fax: 1-614-755-5645.

For Canada order enquiries: please contact McGraw-Hill Ryerson
Ltd, 300 Water St, Whitby, Ontario L1N 9B6, Canada.
Telephone: 905 430 5000. Fax: 905 430 5020.

Long renowned as the authoritative source for self-guided
learning – with more than 50 million copies sold worldwide –
the *Teach Yourself* series includes over 500 titles in the fields of
languages, crafts, hobbies, business, computing and education.

British Library Cataloguing in Publication Data:
a catalogue record for this title is available from the British Library.

Library of Congress Catalog Card Number: on file.

First published in UK 2008 by Hodder Education, part of
Hachette UK, 338 Euston Road, London NW1 3BH.

First published in US 2008 by The McGraw-Hill Companies, Inc.

This edition published 2010.

Previously published as *Teach Yourself Etiquette and Modern
Manners*.

The *Teach Yourself* name is a registered trade mark of
Hodder Headline.

Typeset by MPS Limited, A Macmillan Company.

Printed in Great Britain for Hodder Education, an Hachette UK
Company, 338 Euston Road, London NW1 3BH, by CPI Cox &
Wyman, Reading, Berkshire RG1 8EX.

The publisher has used its best endeavours to ensure that the URLs
for external websites referred to in this book are correct and active
at the time of going to press. However, the publisher and the
author have no responsibility for the websites and can make no
guarantee that a site will remain live or that the content will remain
relevant, decent or appropriate.

Hachette UK's policy is to use papers that are natural, renewable
and recyclable products and made from wood grown in sustainable
forests. The logging and manufacturing processes are expected to
conform to the environmental regulations of the country of origin.

Impression number   10 9 8 7 6 5 4 3 2 1
Year   2014 2013 2012 2011 2010

For Monica, Winston, Sandra, Sarah, Stephen and Nicola, who will never be the most proper people, but are certainly the most loved.

Acknowledgements

Thanks must be given to the authors' friends and family for their constant support and display of etiquette in the real world: Sara McCorquodale and Sonia Dzivane for inspiration and countless words of encouragement; Rachel Boyd for a lifetime's instruction on the birds, bees and friendship; Anna Burdon-Cooper for always being on the other end of a well-mannered mobile phone conversation; Vivienne Blackstone for the late-night supply of fudge; Monica Young for seeing the calm beyond the storm; Nicki Manomaiudom and Elena Andreicheva for their constant forgiveness for lateness; Sarah Harding and Sandra Higgins for their infinite knowledge of everything from barbeques to work dos; Nicola Young for always dissolving tears into giggles; and to James Fisher without whom the authors would never have met, had several terribly polite conversations and written a book.

Image credits

Front cover: © Photodisc/Jupiter Images

Back cover: © Jakub Semeniuk/iStockphoto.com, © Royalty-Free/ Corbis, © agencyby/iStockphoto.com, © Andy Cook/ iStockphoto.com, © Christopher Ewing/iStockphoto.com, © zebicho – Fotolia.com, © Geoffrey Holman/iStockphoto.com, © Photodisc/Getty Images, © James C. Pruitt/iStockphoto.com, © Mohamed Saber – Fotolia.com

Contents

Meet the authors

Welcome to *Be Charming*!

We think that a lot of people are rude. We don't think it's deliberate, but nonetheless we think they're rude. We've all come across it: that woman who doesn't think to move her bag from the only spare seat on the train, that man who mentions that a lady he hasn't seen in a while has put on weight, or that teenager who merrily carries on his mobile phone conversation while paying for an item at a cashier. Even our friends do it occasionally – people we really like.

But wouldn't the world be a much nicer a place to live in if they didn't?

A few of these slips can be cringed at and brushed over, but a lot of them repeatedly would probably stop us wanting to be associated with these people.

However, there is a way to immunize yourself from being slip-up-prone. We believe that manners are skills to be learned and practised – it's a bit like learning a new language. If you practise daily with your family, friends, colleagues, clients and strangers you can watch their respect for you grow.

No book can cover every possible modern-day situation, so instead this one gives guidelines for the most common and most confusing everyday circumstances. And once you understand the reasoning behind these tricks of charm, the rest starts to seem natural.

We think that polite behaviour, particularly in a world where many do not bother with it, distinguishes a person as kind, thoughtful, and intelligent enough to realize that kind and thoughtful behaviour wins friends and business.

Only got a minute?

Being charming requires daily practice. Here are some steps that you can use right now! Try them out today.

Use the words 'please', 'thank you' and 'sorry' liberally, as well as 'good morning', 'good afternoon' and 'good evening'.

Be on time. Don't assume that someone else's time is less valuable than your own. If you are going to be late, warn the other person as early as possible.

Keep yourself clean and tidy. Make a decision to wash your hands more regularly throughout the day. Use soap and lather for at least 15 seconds, paying attention to your fingernails and the backs of your hands.

Be mindful that your body language may be betraying feelings that someone with good manners wouldn't express. Whole books have been written on the topic of body language, but for starters try the following:

▶ Be aware of other people's personal space. For example, don't drape yourself over a chair that someone else is sitting on. If someone takes a step back, don't automatically take a step forward.

▶ What are your arms doing? For example, when trying to be welcoming and approachable, don't cross your arms.

▶ And your facial expression? Don't scowl when you are asked a favour or given a task you dislike.

Think for a moment about your friends and family. Does your established routine have a fair distribution of duties? Does everyone have their personal space respected? Is there anyone you have really been meaning to call? It can become easy to take the people closest to you for granted. Now is the time to make an effort and be charming for them too.

5 Only got five minutes?

Being charming requires daily practice. Here are some steps that you can use this week! Try them out as soon as possible.

Mobile phone etiquette – the essentials

▶ *When around others, turn your phone off or put it on vibrate. Prioritize the person you are with.*
▶ *Do not shout.*
▶ *Remember to observe rules banning mobile phones in some areas.*
▶ *At work, take your phone with you when you leave your desk.*
▶ *Think carefully about the appropriateness of the message when deciding whether to text or call.*

Office etiquette – the essentials

▶ *Don't have conversations across open-plan offices. You will disturb others. Either walk over or use the phone.*
▶ *Keep your desk tidy and regularly cleaned out.*
▶ *Take care of your personal appearance and hygiene.*
▶ *Use your work email address for work email. Prioritize work emails over chit-chat with friends.*
▶ *Try to resolve problems with colleagues directly before involving your boss.*

City survival – the essentials

▶ *Be mindful of others in a rush and be mindful of others when you are in a rush.*

- *Stop your bags bashing into people.*
- *Where possible, take the stairs at times when lifts are likely to be busy.*
- *Smile at strangers on public transport but do not insist upon conversation if it seems unwelcome.*
- *Give up your seat on public transport to those who need it more than you.*

In a car – the essentials

- *Periodically refresh your knowledge of The Highway Code, which contains the definitive guide for good behaviour on the road.*
- *Keep your temper, despite the bad driving of others. Horns should be used only as a warning and never as a vent for road rage.*
- *Litter should never be thrown out of the window of a moving vehicle, even if the item is biodegradable.*
- *During the trip, music choices should accommodate the tastes of everyone in the car.*
- *As a passenger, keep backseat driving to a minimum.*

General tips!

- *If in doubt about whether to tip, tip.*
- *Leave bathrooms the way you found them.*
- *When people try to have a conversation with you, remove the earphones of your music player.*
- *Don't jump queues.*
- *Don't swear in public.*
- *Use the words 'please', 'thank you' and 'sorry' liberally.*
- *Always stand your round in bars.*
- *Be on time.*
- *Give compliments generously and receive them modestly.*

10 Only got ten minutes?

Being charming requires practice. Here is an analysis of ten modern-day dilemmas. Use these solutions the next time these situations arise.

Meeting for the first time – handshake or kiss?

A good first rule here is to do the same as the people you see around you. Men should generally shake hands for the first two meetings and then avoid the ritual altogether. Offer a hand to a lady and wait to see if she leans in for a kiss. For women, some feel comfortable with kissing from the start. However, remember that air kissing is always a little too impersonal to be friendly.

At a party – how do I get away from this person/ conversation?

Try your hardest not to leave someone standing on their own. But if you must leave, leave politely: apologize, give a reason for leaving and then move away. Alternatively, use a line such as 'I've been monopolizing you' or 'I've taken up enough of your time', which shifts the implied blame for boredom onto yourself.

Mobile phones – to text or not to text?

- ▶ *Is the message likely to provoke an emotional reaction? If so, always call.*
- ▶ *Is a call likely to disrupt people on either your end of the line or the recipients'? If so, text.*
- ▶ *Will more than one text be required to clarify the situation? If so, call.*

> ► *Is the person likely to want to retain the information for reference (for example, directions)? If so, text.*

Dinner parties – what should I cook?

Cook a dish that you believe your guests will want to eat, not one that showcases your own culinary tastes and skills. Also, cook something that you are practised at – now is not the time to try a soufflé if you have never attempted one before. Prepare dishes so there is minimal fuss between courses. Always cook more than you think will be needed. If you know that one of your guests has an allergy, change what you had planned to serve to everyone in order to avoid using that ingredient. If disaster strikes, be prepared with the telephone number of a good takeaway.

At work – do I have to contribute to birthday collections?

If your company is large (more than 40 people) then you don't need to contribute to every birthday/new baby/leaving present collection. If you don't know the person, you do not need to open your wallet. But if you do know the person well enough to say hello to, give to the collection. The amount will depend on your workplace so try to gauge what is normal.

Personal appearance – what exactly is smart casual?

For men this means that you need a collar of some sort, whether it be a polo shirt or a proper shirt. Although the definition will vary according to age and occasion, it is safer to wear proper shoes (not trainers or flip flops) and a pair of full length trousers not made of denim. No tie should be worn – a jumper (not a hoody) or a cardigan will suffice, and a jacket may be worn. For women, this means slightly more decorative dress than 'casual' attire. Simply avoid denim, trainers and hoodies.

Restaurants – how do I choose the wine?

The old rule of white wine with white meat and red with red no longer strictly applies with today's blends, so this decision has become more complex in recent years. Feel free to delegate this responsibility or to ask the wine waiter for their assistance. If the people around your table are ordering many different kinds of food, consider ordering by the glass or ordering red and white. If you know about wine, keep your deliberations short – nobody likes a wine bore.

Pubs/bars – can I have … ?

Always stand your round. If you cannot afford to do this, you can't afford to be there. Buying a round is not simply a matter of stumping up the cash, it is also a matter of effort. The round-buyer must battle with the bar queues and act as waiter. Don't shout, whistle or gesticulate wildly at a barman to demand service. Attention-seeking gestures must be limited to a raise of the hand, not higher than shoulder-height, eye contact and perhaps a raise of the eyebrows. Money can be held in a hand clearly visible to the bar staff, but do not wave it – you are in a bar, not a strip club.

Coming out – how do I react?

When a gay person comes out to you, your reaction to the situation is important. The words 'are you sure?' should not cross your lips. Of course, they're sure. Do not immediately ask difficult questions such as those about religion, their prospects of having children or whether they are out to their family. If you are used to hugging this person, do so now and make an extra effort to mantain regular contact for the first few months after the coming-out.

Relationships – how do I deflect a chat-up?

If someone chats you up, be nice about it – it took guts to come up to you. Lie if you have to and say you're sorry (lie), they seem brilliant (lie) and in other circumstances you would (lie), but you're seeing someone at the moment (lie lie lie), or you've just broken up with someone (lie), or you're just really not looking for someone in your life for a while (lie). Be polite while making your feelings clear. If someone turns you down, take the hint. Gather your pride, say 'that's a shame' and go back to your friends who delight in your company.

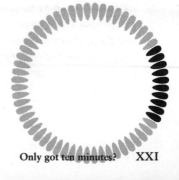

Introduction

No more is it enough to cast a coat over a puddle for a lady to pass without dampening her feet, or for a woman to know the correct direction and angle at which to cross her legs. In the current day minefield of blogging, office romances and shenanigans worthy of our grandmother's blushes, the handbook of social niceties is long overdue an update.

The western world is one of fast-paced expressiveness and almost forced informality. This, however, does not automatically exclude its inhabitants from the practice of manners and etiquette, in fact it is precisely the terms of this world which demand it – manners are always more noticeable and impressive in company where they are not habitually used. In addition, with the vast number of people comes a catalogue of sexualities, fetishes, eating habits and living situations, and seemingly limitless opportunities to unintentionally cause personal offence.

To make matters worse, the sudden and rapid growth of technology has left the everyday blogger without any established formal code of netiquette. An iPod sadly does not come with iManners included. Mobile phones are essential but when is it inappropriate to text rather than talk?

Most of us think we know how to act. Be nice and don't mug old ladies, kick kittens or pass wind in confined areas. But those are easy. What do you do with your chopsticks when you have finished eating? Is it okay to send a formal thank-you note by email or even instant message? Some may think these questions indicate the decline of civilized society, while others may think manners and etiquette are changing with evolving technology and societal expectations. There may be some occasions where it is impossible to please all, but this book standardizes currently fashionable etiquette and modern manners, giving a basis which, where possible, errs on the side of inoffensive to the majority in the early twenty-first century.

Ethics and etiquette are frequently confused, and fairly so as they are heavily entwined. Etiquette is often learned as a part of ethics, as a sign of respect. However, there is an evident difference between the two – one has all the goodness and the other all the appearance of it. Learning from this book may not in itself prevent you from descending into evil and all its vices, minding ps and qs down the fiery ladder, but it is certainly a good place to start.

In the following chapters you will find advice on a range of topics including: how to create a good first impression, how to get on with your work colleagues, how to share a house successfully, the etiquette rules of modern technology such as emailing and texting as well as the rules of modern dating and how to be a good host, to name but a few.

It should be remembered, though, that modern etiquette is not about laying down rigid rules. The regular practice of modern etiquette is simply a reminder to those who bother with it to be thoughtful and considerate without having to expend the creative effort of coming up with their own method of doing so each and every time. It's the lazy way to be perfectly polite.

1

Introductions

In this chapter you will learn how to:
* *make introductions*
* *tackle the problem of forgetting a name*
* *handshake or kiss*
* *network.*

The value of a good introduction

You stand at the edge of the crowd. Smoothly, you glide towards
the only person you know and they turn to greet you happily.
They then continue with the joke/story/gossiping/inanely dull
conversation your arrival interrupted. You are not introduced.
The group glances curiously at you but sadly without an
introduction you barely exist, you are merely another object in the
room, much the same as a beautiful chandelier hanging from the
ceiling (if you are blessed with good looks) or an ornamental floor
rug (if you are not). With the right introduction, you could have
sparkled and joined in with your own killer line about the traffic
on the way here, or maybe have even felt comfortable enough to
start with that aunt-camel-priest joke you've been dying to tell.
But sadly it is not to be.

The importance of introductions is not merely the provision of a
name. No one cares what your name actually is, unless it really
is something devastatingly unusual, in which case it may serve as

a conversation starter. Most, as rude as it may be, will forget it almost instantly. In its barest form, an introduction is the accepted method by which the introducer, who knows the two people to be introduced, vouches for the character of the introducees by having a prior acquaintance. The level of enthusiasm with which the introducer takes on the task is indicative of the relationship between the introducer and the newcomer, so if you are the one saddled with the task, take it on with gusto. The newcomer will be delighted you think so highly of them and anyone to which you make the introduction will immediately believe the person to whom they are being introduced is worthy of their time and conversational skills.

WHEN THE 'INTRODUCER' FORGETS TO INTRODUCE

Occasionally, the go-between will forget to introduce. At this point, if you are a friend of the go-between, the kindest thing to do is to loudly and jokingly force him/her into an introduction of the newcomer. The go-between should, at this point, apologize emphatically for their misbehaviour and make a greater effort to incorporate them into the conversation.

Insight

Do not insist that the introducer give the name of the person who has joined the group, just in case they are unsure of it. Instead, jokingly hold your own hand out and say 'Hi, I'm [insert name]'.

How to make an introduction

When making an introduction, the level of formality will inevitably depend upon the circumstances under which the introduction is taking place. However, a few general rules can be applied to any situation.

When making an introduction, try not to mumble or look away. It gives the impression of disinterest and makes it difficult to hear.

Timing is important. Wait for the first available pause to introduce someone. By all means interrupt your own chatter to introduce a person. In fact, providing that you are not about to deliver the short and sharp punchline of a very long joke, this is the perfect moment, as it will give the impression that your delight in introducing the newcomer far outweighs any trivial point you may have been labouring. Conversation has a convenient way of naturally slowing as an introduction seems imminent; however, if it does not, try not to interrupt another person's chatter with an introduction. Instead wait for a breath and dive in with a confident 'Do you know John Smith?'

In the modern world, common practice uses either a first name only or first name and surname introduction. This is, by and large, acceptable, but in formal settings, or when introducing someone elderly or in a position of power, it is wise to introduce them as Mr/Mrs/Miss/Lord/Lady/Sir Smith, and let the person introduced make the preferred adjustment. If in doubt, err on the side of formality and do it with confidence. Better to be a prude than rude.

Insight

When introducing yourself, in personal situations use your first name only, adding detail about your relation to the event. In business situations, use your first name, last name and company name. Omit your business title as it sounds ridiculous if you are low in a company and pompous if you are high.

Married couples should be introduced individually. However, bear in mind that sometimes married women choose to keep their surname, and if this is the case it is sensible to add the detail 'John's wife' or 'Jane's husband'. When introducing family or close friends, try to incorporate the link into the introduction, for example, 'Anna, have you met my sister Rachel?'

Traditionally, most importantly, men are introduced to women and secondly, juniors to seniors. (If A is introduced to B, A's name goes second in the introduction, for example, 'B, it is my pleasure to introduce A'.) Socially, in a formal setting or if an older generation is involved, people tend to stick roughly to this rule. However, these days, an introduction is largely made between two people as equals, even if this is to some extent pretence, with no regard to age or gender. For the etiquette of business introductions, see page 32.

Try your hardest to remember names. Nobody likes to be forgettable, even if you only met them for three seconds blind drunk five years ago. If they can remember you, it will be offensive if you cannot remember them. If loss of memory strikes frequently, train partners and friends to become skilled in the art of recognizing your discomfort, for example, by using a key word, at which point they can leap to the rescue by introducing themselves and forcing a self-introduction from the other party. Failing that, bluff. If you must introduce someone whose name you do not know, use a moderate level of enthusiasm, just in case you are caught out, and plump for the 'Have you met [insert name]' one-sided approach. If caught, feign early senility, ill health or a traumatic day at the dentist/work/home. If you cannot recall either name for the introduction, duck out of the conversation immediately before you are forced into making an introduction.

Also, try to remember something about the person you introduce which may act as a conversation starter between the two people. This may also help with a name block. Almost anything will do: their hobbies, where they live, what they do for a living, who they know or if they had a difficult journey to the event.

People draw conclusions about each other from the first few seconds of meeting. Of course, first impressions can be changed with time and prolonged exposure, but it is likely that if your first impression is not a positive one then the time and prolonged exposure required to change that opinion may not be available. Stand up and be aware of your posture, engage in eye contact and smile. This response to an introduction gives the other person the idea that you are interested in them, you are ready to welcome or join them in conversation and that you are seeing them as an equal – all qualities regarded as good manners.

Handshake or kiss?

Depending on the circumstances, either a kiss or handshake may be appropriate. This, however, often ends in the swallowing of hair or the impression of forced formality. Good observational skills and fast reflexes are the only fail-safe method, but socially there are some guidelines as follows.

When men greet each other, they should handshake on the first two meetings and then subsequently avoid the ritual altogether. If one or more women are involved, the greeting should take the form of shaking hands on first meeting and then kissing upon any subsequent meeting – one or two is a matter of personal preference.

There are such diverse cultures even within a single country that it is near impossible to get it right all the time, and even if you do, that person may have adjusted their regional or national habits to suit your own. However air kissing is always a little too impersonal to be friendly, so aim for skin.

Men should never insist upon a kiss at a first meeting. Offer a hand for a handshake and let the lady draw you near for a kiss if they choose. In some circumstances, women feel comfortable kissing each other from the start. The only real rule is not to take offence if your idea of a suitable greeting has not been adhered to. Personal space is a subjective idea, and some imaginary circles are smaller than others. Bear this in mind and judge the situation accordingly.

In unfamiliar groups or situations, it is always advisable to copy the actions of others. Modern manners and etiquette are about fitting in and not causing a scene. Observe the kissing or shaking habits of a group and prepare yourself for similar treatment.

How to execute the perfect handshake

Many people believe handshakes to be an indicator of personality. Violently shake or squeeze too hard and you'll be branded aggressive; put forward a limp hand, you'll be thought of as weak; over-shake at the risk of seeming irritating and clingy. Of course, give a nice, normal handshake and you'll be expected to be, well, normal. For a normal handshake:

1 *Make sure your palms are not sweaty – (wipe palms quickly before shaking if necessary).*
2 *Face your handshake partner.*
3 *Use your right hand (the only exception to this is if a right hand does not exist).*
4 *The web between your thumb and first finger should touch the same part of the other person's hand (see Figure 1.1).*
5 *Use pressure similar to how you would grip an empty fizzy drink can just before it crushes.*
6 *Pump between one and three times.*
7 *Smile throughout.*

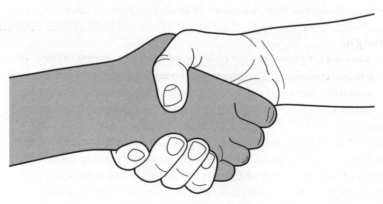

Figure 1.1 *The web between your thumb and first finger should touch the same part of the other person's hand.*

If you come hand to hand with a non-normal handshake, go with
the flow and try not to grimace. If a person seems to want to shake
for longer than you expect, don't take your hand away early, hold
on until the natural release comes.

Insight

Wait for your moment. Try not to interrupt someone
completely engaged in conversation to shake a hand. If you
are meeting someone for the first time, shaking hands is a
good opportunity to introduce yourself.

Networking events

In the most nightmarish of situations, the cut-throat networking
event, PR people are often brought in specifically for the task
of making introductions. However, they are limited and busy.
Introduce yourself to as many people as possible. It is what you
are there to do. Shake hands and distribute business cards, if you
have them, at the start of a conversation to clarify your name. Fear
nobody and embrace the power of the name tag. You have been
invited to the event, you already belong.

Insight

Take an ample supply of cards to networking events. Offer
one immediately upon meeting someone new. When taking
someone else's card, study the name carefully and try to use it
as soon as possible as it will help you remember it later.

Do not be insulted when the person with whom you are speaking
makes a short sharp excuse and turns to introduce themselves
to another person. It is what they are there to do, too. At a
networking event, however, by far the best way of extricating
yourself from a conversation is to introduce the person to someone
whom you know, then duck away. Unlike social parties, at

networking events, it is acceptable to leave someone on their own, but it is not nice to do so without a reason. So, before you attend the event, think through some good parting comments such as, 'I'm so sorry, but I must use the rest room', or 'I'm just going to hunt down a refill', or 'I've just seen [insert name], I must grab them for a quick chat now before they leave' or even just 'I've taken up too much of your time for an occasion such as this – there are others that you must meet'. Do whatever your excuse stated quickly or at least move out of the sight of the person you have left, before returning to speak to someone else.

Insight

After networking events, write on the back of each card as much as you can remember about the owner of the card to help your memory should they be in touch.

10 THINGS TO REMEMBER

1 *Always introduce people who are strangers to each other, even if you don't know them well.*

2 *Err on the side of formality in presenting the name.*

3 *When shaking hands, face your handshake partner and extend your right hand.*

4 *When using a kiss as a greeting, aim to touch cheeks or go lip to cheek. Air kissing is pretentious.*

5 *At networking events, do not monopolize one person's time.*

6 *Try to make introductions with some comment that can act as a conversation starter.*

7 *Encourage others to make introductions.*

8 *Introductions serve as an entry into conversation.*

9 *Use eye contact with both the introducer and the group when introducing.*

10 *Never take offence if your idea of a suitable greeting has not been followed.*

2

The art of making conversation

In this chapter you will learn how to:
- *choose a topic of conversation*
- *answer the question 'How are you?'*
- *extricate yourself politely from a conversation.*

Suitable topics for conversation

Hopefully, during the process of introduction you will have been given leeway into a natural topic of conversation. However, if this is not the case, you may have to create the initial spark of chit-chat yourself.

Begin by asking questions. Most people, because of their undeniable authority on the matter, find it easiest to talk about themselves and their experiences. Beware of questions that are too personal, such as health or relationship troubles, and lean towards subjects such as places the person has been to or what football team they support. You already have something in common by being in the same place with the same people, so if stuck, simply comment on your surroundings and ask if they agree, or ask how the other person knows the hosts. Another alternative is to find something about the person that you admire, and compliment it, asking for further details.

Insight

Where possible, do some background research on the people you know you will be meeting. It will be easier to find an interesting topic of conversation if you already have some idea of what the other person may find interesting, or is working on at that time.

Try to set the tone of the conversation to match the mood of the event. If it is a sombre occasion, don't talk about your previous evening's one-night stand. If it is a light-hearted cocktail party, don't dampen the mood by talking about your fears that your wife is cheating on you.

If talking in a group, try not to focus on a topic of conversation that will only be interesting to a few. For example, when talking to a work colleague and his or her spouse, don't talk about the details of business that cannot be followed or be interesting to the spouse.

If throughout the flow of a conversation you hit upon a topic that clearly makes one or more of your group uncomfortable, change the subject immediately and retreat to safer ground, such as sport, the news, your surroundings, the town or a film or television programme. The list of safer topics is endless but the list of acknowledged risky subjects is quite short.

Insight

Keep on top of current affairs. News topics are easy to talk about as they are by nature either remarkable or subjects which spark debate.

Try to avoid the following:

▶ **Money** – *Chatter about money has a tendency to make everyone feel uncomfortable as it forces people to think of how much or little they have themselves, and will make the person talking about it seem obsessed with the stuff – not an attractive quality. Never ask how much a stranger earns or volunteer your own salary for scrutiny. Only ask friends* *in private and if it serves a particular purpose, such as determining whether you are underpaid. Don't talk about the financial situations of others, or the lending or borrowing of money. In most conversational topics, the mention of money is merely a descriptive detail which can be omitted. Endeavour to do so.*

▶ **Sex** – *Although there are many people, particularly of the younger generation, who feel comfortable talking about sex in public, there are many who will find this chatter crude. Because it is such a private affair, what you may find normal another may find repulsive and vice versa. As well as staying off the topic of the act itself, it is wise to also stay off the topic of adultery (either your own or a third party's) as you really have no idea what everyone listening is up to, or indeed who knows whom.*

▶ **Recent surgery or health problems** – *There are very few people in the world who genuinely will be interested in the surgical procedure of removing an ingrowing toenail. Neither are there people whose deepest desire is to find out the symptoms of your latest flu. No matter the disease, you are likely to put your conversational partner off food for the rest of the day if you carry on along these lines. If you have been noticeably unwell recently, respond to questions about your health with positive comments such as 'not very well recently but I'm sure I'm on the mend now'.*

Exercise caution when talking about the following:

▶ **Politics** – *As fun as lively debates may be, it is wise to remember that voting is a deliberately and elaborately secret process and, in the spirit of that tradition, some may be unwilling to reveal which side of the political fence they sit on. These people are acutely aware that upon declaring yourself a devout follower of one political party, you reveal much about yourself, as your way of thinking is likely to mirror that of your vote. In addition, it may give clues as to how you were brought up – personal information that you may prefer not to share. Bear this reluctance in mind and remember that* *although some ferociously defend their political stance, there are others who will find this sort of confrontation abhorrent.*

▶ *If you are desperate for intellectual debate, you may try to activate this topic of conversation with close friends who are aware that it is merely a debate rather than a judgement on their character. However, in company with which you are less familiar, talking about political parties is quite simply too personal for polite party patter.*

▶ **Religion** – *Similarly, during a lifetime you are likely to meet people ranging from those who are determined to tell you all about their religion to those who want to keep their tarot cards close to their chest. Religion has caused some people to do very good things and others very bad things. Belief is an elaborately complicated affair and challenging a person's faith is likely to look more like a mockery or attack than pure interest. For those who do manage to frame questions in such a way that expresses interest rather than condemnation, remember that the person may be finding it tiring acting as an unelected spokesperson of their faith, particularly if that faith has recently been under media scrutiny. Look for signs that the other person may want to change the subject, and act immediately if this is apparent.*

Answering the question 'How are you?'

This question is a civility. It is not a question requiring a thoughtful answer. The response 'Fine, how are you?' should come as a reflex action. Do not tell the other person about your imminent divorce, your health troubles or your work issues in response. If you have been truly suffering in some way, say, 'Not so great recently but everything's getting back on track now', and wait to be prompted if the person does indeed want to hear more. If everything really is hunky-dory in your life and you want to talk about a positive issue, do so briefly or you will seem as though you are gloating. If you have children, be aware that a monologue lasting over two minutes about their merits and troubles is also unlikely to win you friends.

Last but not least, you must ask the 'How are you?' question back within a few minutes.

THE EXCEPTION OF FRIENDSHIP

Of course, the above are only guidelines for topics of conversation in public or with strangers or recent acquaintances. In private, with close friends (or a therapist), the sky's the limit. It's up to you to determine what your friends will or will not be comfortable talking about, but always remember when dealing with either close friends or strangers to change the subject quickly if the other person shows signs of negative emotion and discomfort with that negative emotion.

Commenting on change

No matter how close you may be to a person, never comment on changes in appearance unless the change is clearly a positive one and is likely to be thought of as such by the changed person.

Insight
When you receive a compliment, accept it with grace. Say thank you.

When you are uncomfortable with a topic of conversation

You may refuse to answer questions if you believe that they are too personal or may provoke an emotional response within yourself. Simply smile and say 'I'm sorry, I don't feel comfortable answering that' or, 'No comment' and change the topic to something safer. If, however, you are simply being subjected to a boring monologue, you must simply wait it out for at least ten minutes until it is possible to politely extricate yourself. If you find the monologue offensive, change the topic or explain your distaste and wait for an apology. If the apology does not come, change the topic or leave the conversation as soon as possible.

Balancing conversation

Remember that conversation is a game for two or more people, not a solo affair. Listen properly and ask thoughtful, relevant questions. By doing this, make sure that the person you are speaking to is talking as much or more than you are. Look at the person and maintain eye contact; don't look around to see if there is anyone more interesting or better looking to speak to and don't gaze at the floor or the ceiling.

Insight

Eye contact is important for conversation. Maintain it as much as possible to let the other person know you are interested in what they have to say.

Extricating yourself from conversation

Try your hardest not to leave someone standing on their own. However, if the conversation really has become unbearable (and you must have been speaking to the person for a minimum of ten minutes for this to be discernible) or you do need to leave, be polite in your leaving. Apologize, give a reason for departing from the conversation (such as needing to visit the rest room) and then move, having shaken hands or touched an arm to maintain the idea of newfound closeness. Alternatively, use a line such as, 'I've been monopolizing you' or 'I've taken up enough of your time', thus shifting the implied blame for boredom onto yourself.

10 THINGS TO REMEMBER

1 *Ask general, open-ended questions that give your conversation partner room to talk.*

2 *Set the tone of the conversation to match the mood of the event.*

3 *Focus on topics that will be interesting to a whole group; rather than just a select few.*

4 *Avoid overly personal questions in group settings, or when speaking to someone you are unfamiliar with.*

5 *To be safe, avoid talking about money, sex and health problems.*

6 *Try to add a positive lilt to conversations – find the silver lining.*

7 *Exercise caution when talking about politics and religion.*

8 *If you find a topic of conversation offensive, try to change it at least twice before saying so.*

9 *Listen and try to ensure the person you are speaking to is speaking as much as yourself.*

10 *Try not to leave someone standing on their own – where possible make introductions to another person before extricating yourself.*

3

Mobile phone etiquette

In this chapter you will learn how to:
- *choose between vibrate, silent or ring functions for a variety of situations*
- *take a call in public*
- *leave an answerphone message*
- *decide whether to send a text or make a phone call.*

Mobile phones are one of the true blessings and curses of modern living. Even that dwindling crowd who reject this form of communication suffer and benefit from the mobile phone's permeation of society. That device which creates a phantom proximity of emergency services and friends on a dark walk home often alienates us from the people with whom we share a physical space.

When to take a call

Although most mobile phone users now understand that in some circumstances answering a phone is as much a social faux pas as plucking your armpit hair in public, there remains confusion as to which circumstances create this outrage. In addition, the various functions of texting, emailing and calling, silent modes and choice of ringtone all add to the obstacle course of mobile phone manners. To vibrate or not to vibrate, that is the pulsating question of the day.

Expectant fathers will always be forgiven for taking a call from their wife or partner and doctors on call are accepted prisoners of their mobiles. There may be exceptions and no list of rules can compete with a general consideration of the feelings of others. Think of the following as a starting point.

SILENCE IS GOLDEN

▶ *When around others, if you cannot turn your phone off, put it on silent and/or vibrate.*
▶ *In meetings and conferences, put your phone on silent or preferably turn it off. Remember that in quiet environments the buzzing of the vibrate mode is audible. To some people that buzzing is as irritating as an infestation of killer bees. Never leave a mobile phone on vibrate on a table, you may as well have left the ringtone on.*
▶ *If the call cannot be ignored, exit the room to speak.*
▶ *At work, take your phone with you if you leave your desk. Mobile phones, though they may be used for business, are considered personal property, so few colleagues will venture to answer it or hang up on the caller even if 'I will survive' is blaring out for the sixth time in 15 minutes.*

DURING MEETINGS

▶ *In smaller meetings, if you are awaiting an important call which may necessitate your leaving the room hastily, explain briefly and apologize at the start before it happens.*
▶ *In restaurants, phones should be turned off, or if absolutely necessary, on vibrate with the ringtone switched off. The phone should be kept in your pocket and not on the table. Out of courtesy for those you are with, do not accept calls or texts at the table. If absolutely necessary, take it outside and keep it short.*
▶ *Prioritize the person you are with. With all things being equal, the person you are with is more important than the person on the end of a phone. If you receive a call during a conversation, send the call to voicemail and wait for your company to finish their speech on the history of buttons, or whatever. If the call is likely*

to be urgent or the caller is persistent, apologize to the person you are with (preferably with a comment implying that you would much rather continue your scintillating banter with them) and take the call, but keep it as brief as possible, explaining that you are with company. Take the urgent information and offer to call back for the conversational padding. When the call is over, again apologize to everyone at the table.

IN PUBLIC

▶ *It is not possible to pay for items politely at a cashier while having a phone clamped to one ear.*
▶ *Telephones have come a long way from the days of a string connecting two cups. Mobile phones make it unnecessary to shout. The microphones on those things are remarkably sensitive so keep your voice down.*
▶ *People's sense of aural personal space varies from situation to situation. In busy places where it is difficult to distinguish one voice from the general background chatter, it is normally thought acceptable to speak at length, if need be, on a mobile. Talking loudly in a confined public space such as a lift or train carriage is not. If possible, use a text message instead for these situations.*
▶ *Don't argue in public on mobile phones. It gives the impression of having an argument with yourself and if you are arguing with a particularly stupid person the effect will be even worse.*
▶ *Bluetooth headsets look daft and talking into them makes you look like a madman. Use them when you need them and take them off when you don't. Buy a hands-free set if you want to use your mobile while driving or riding a bicycle. It is a breach of etiquette to kill people.*

WHERE MOBILE PHONES ARE BANNED

Never chatter on a mobile phone in lifts, libraries, museums, restaurants, cemeteries, theatres, cinemas, dentist or doctor waiting rooms or places of worship. Keep conversation to a minimum and at a low volume in any enclosed public spaces, such as buses and trains. Bear in mind that everyone on the train already knows you are on the train.

If a mobile phone call is taken in a designated mobile-phone-free area (identified by a prominently displayed sign), politely explain to the user that they need to take the call outside. They may not have noticed signs indicating that mobile phones are unwanted.

Other functions of the phone

If you are going to play games on your mobile, turn off the button noises and the sound. Your top score on Tetris should be a private achievement.

Respect the privacy of others when using a camera phone. In-phone cameras should not be used anywhere a normal camera would be considered inappropriate, such as in changing rooms or toilets. Ask for permission before you take someone's picture. Pretending to use a phone function while actually taking a photo of someone will fool nobody. Remember that paparazzi are often punched.

CHOOSE YOUR RINGTONE WISELY

The best choice is perhaps a ringtone that sounds like a domestic phone. Although boring, it is the least irritating should your mobile ring inappropriately. Fifteen-second clips of Westlife will not add to your street cred anyway.

Answerphone etiquette

If the call is important enough to leave a message, then explain the purpose of your call as well as leaving your name. 'Call me back' is not enough information for the person to gauge the level of urgency required in returning the call.

Your phone is not a weapon

Don't send inappropriate, offensive or threatening voice, text or picture messages. Apart from it being illegal to harass someone in this manner, it's just not very nice, is it?

Mobile phone basics

Although the points raised above may seem lengthy, remembering a few basics is all that is really needed. Before reaching for your phone in public, remember the following:

▶ *It is only in very rare circumstances that world destruction will occur if you neglect to answer a mobile phone at the precise instant when it first rings. In the event of the caller ringing to warn of imminent doom and destruction, they are probably wise enough to leave a message.*
▶ *The clever phone people invented the off switch, a silent mode and a vibrate function so that you could use them.*
▶ *Your mobile phone is not magical and cannot make you inaudible to the outside world or prevent you from irritating others.*

Texting versus calling

There are many situations where a text is as welcome as a call, but when considering which to do, think of the following in order of declining importance:

▶ *Is the message likely to provoke an emotional reaction? If so, always call.*
▶ *Is a call likely to disrupt people on either your end of the line or the recipients? If so, text.*

► *Will more than one text be required to clarify the situation? If so call.*

► *Is the person likely to want to retain the information for reference (for example directions)? If so, text.*

Do not send text messages in meetings or conferences – it is the adult equivalent of passing notes in class. In addition, don't forget that speakers act as an alarm system for such messaging, popping out that radio signal just when you thought you'd got away with that crafty one-handed text in your pocket.

Since the invention and widespread use of predictive texting, there is no longer any need to write in abbreviated txt-spk for ease of communication, as it is far quicker to use the former. If you simply can't bear to give it up entirely, continue to do so but only use abbreviations such as 'c u l8r', that are obvious or widely known, as over-use of text speak may make your text at best difficult to read and at worst indecipherable.

Insight

It is easier to read a text than pick up a mobile phone's voicemail. If you call and are redirected to answerphone, send a text if your message is short enough to convey the full meaning and is appropriate for texting.

10 THINGS TO REMEMBER

1 *When around others, turn your phone off or put it on vibrate.*

2 *If a call cannot be ignored, exit a room full of people to speak.*

3 *At work, take your phone with you when you leave your desk.*

4 *Keep phones in your pocket on vibrate, not on restaurant tables.*

5 *When possible, prioritize the person you are with.*

6 *Do not shout.*

7 *Keep conversation to a minimum and at low volume in enclosed public spaces.*

8 *Think carefully about the appropriateness of the message when deciding whether to text or call.*

9 *Keep your message decipherable by only using well-known text abbreviations.*

10 *Observe rules banning mobile phones in some areas.*

4

Work etiquette

In this chapter you will learn how to:
- *behave in an office environment*
- *deal with your boss*
- *complain about something at work*
- *conduct an office romance*
- *do business abroad.*

No matter the power hierarchy of bosses and employees, respect through a use of etiquette rather than sycophancy will make a working environment more harmonious.

Welcoming newcomers

It is the duty of the installed office staff to suggest lunch or drinks as an exercise to bond with a newcomer. They should endeavour to do this within the first fortnight of a newcomer's arrival. The newcomer may make noises to colleagues about desiring such a gathering, but should not make specific suggestions as they may unknowingly interrupt a ritual and thus, innocently, cause discontent.

Making the tea

It depends on the office as to what your duties will be regarding kitchen-going. In some places, it is a case of every man for himself; in others, tea drinking is sternly a group activity. Wait for half a day and observe the customs of your office before making yourself, or offering others, a cup. Unless it is strictly the done thing in your office, offering to make just your boss a cup of tea will seem sycophantic. You may as well have announced to the office that it would be a pleasure to lick your master's shoes, pointing wildly at your boss's feet for emphasis.

Office romance

The ever-occurring but ill-advised office romance is often woven with traps that can lose you not only your colleagues' respect but also your job. The best idea of all is simply not to indulge in that raucous pleasure at work, but sometimes it is all too tempting.

If you must go down this route, choose your partner wisely. Think of it as a direct choice between your job and the person you want to get involved with. Most work relationships will at some point end in tears and the two halves will need to deal with the usual range of emotions as well as any sort of fallout resulting from relative positions within a work hierarchy. If you would both willingly lose your jobs or move company for a chance with the other person, follow the guidelines below.

If not, back quickly away.

▶ *Accept that your colleagues will somehow know, but keep it a strong suspicion rather than a determined fact. Keep any romantic office liaisons strictly secret and talk with your partner about the importance of doing so. If it does evolve into a more serious relationship, come to a mutual decision about when to break the pact of secrecy and start mentioning it to colleagues.*
▶ *You are only permitted one dip of your pen in the office ink. If your first office relationship is not successful and the love of your life walks in the next day, tough. Quit if you want to see them, it's not fair on your office-ex any other way.*

- ▶ *At all points, do not do anything at the office with your partner that you would not do with a friend. As funny or appealing as the prospect of hot sex on your desk or a stolen kiss by the water cooler may be, you will likely be spotted and thought of as unprofessional, no matter whether you are married or it is just an ill-advised fling.*
- ▶ *Don't be tempted to send dirty emails or instant messages to work accounts. These forms of communication are monitored by office IT departments and this chatter in most places is a sacking offence.*
- ▶ *If you break a workmate's heart in some hurtful and unforgivable way such as unfaithfulness, consider leaving the company to spare them the pain of having to see you everyday.*

Insight

It is unacceptable to show any form of preference in working life for your partner over other members of staff.

Office politics

Again, the best advice is to steer clear or make an open policy of sitting on the fence. However, if the political situation involves you directly, remember never to shout or hit below the belt and never cause a scene. If the situation is one which may affect your work, call a meeting with your immediate boss to explain your side of the story. Do not bitch or gossip, no matter how tempting.

If you have a grievance with someone, it is better to deal with them directly. Ask to speak to them privately and explain your problem. If you think that you may become emotional, email your grievance, asking for a response.

Remove yourself emotionally from the situation. If you are involved in an argument with someone and feel that you are not making any progress, cool down for a few hours, take a deep breath and email, restating your position coherently and unemotionally. Re-read and send. If you lose your temper, always apologize for that, even if you are in the right in terms of the argument itself.

Clients

Clients should be treated with the respect you afford your boss. As friendly as they may be, the client has the option to say no to you (and your business). Be particularly cautious when considering, for example, how to address them.

At client or contact lunches, whoever did the asking should do the paying. NO exceptions. If your companion is paying, never order the most expensive item on the menu and follow their lead on whether to order alcohol. Talk business only after starters have been finished.

Bonus day

As a general rule, it is considered bad form to talk about money. With regard to wages and bonus pay, this is particularly true when talking with your colleagues. In these matters, if you are asked merely out of the other person's curiosity, you may politely refuse to disclose the sum. On the other hand, if the question has a purpose which has been explained to you, if you consider the person a discreet friend, and if you have no reason for wanting to keep the magic number a secret, then tell them, adding that you insist the information goes no further.

Bonus day is riddled with other non-verbal gestures. In order to survive this most fraught of days (particularly in the City, where bonuses comprise a large portion of each year's pay), practise your poker face. If the result has been good, it will not do your image as a team player any good to boast and if bad, it stings of a bad loser to interrupt the rejoicing of others. As well as keeping a close check on your general demeanour, think carefully about how many post-work drinks to buy at the bar. Be aware of how few some are buying and how others are drinking champagne as though grapes are on a plant extinction list. Aim to hit a target somewhere between the two if you plan to stay under the bonus radar.

Borrowing desk space

Just because the rightful owner of a desk has left spare notebooks/hand-cream/cereal on a desk that you are borrowing does not mean that you also have permission to borrow these. You may borrow a pen if you are desperate, but you must return it. That's it. Think of the drawers of a borrowed office desk as being as off-limits as the top drawer of someone else's bedside table. People tend to keep personal items hidden there and you have no right nosing around.

Leave everything as you found it and don't leave anything extra. Your presence should be indiscernible.

In most offices these days, computers are networked so that anyone with a username and login password can access their desktop from any computer. If you are borrowing a colleague's computer, do not forget to logout when you leave. Many programmes enable an auto-lock feature after a certain period of inactivity where only an administrator or the person logged in may enter the computer. So, by staying logged on, you may accidentally lock the rightful owner of the computer out.

Personal appearance

If you have been given a uniform, wear it well. Keep hair and nails tidy and avoid an excessive use of jewellery. Both boys and girls should be acutely conscious of the number of buttons undone on one's shirt.

For jobs without a set uniform, upon the settlement of a start date for your new job, ask about the office dress code. If you forget to do this, call the person offering the job on the pretence of some other work-related matter, for example preparation reading material, throwing the question of attire in casually.

If it is not possible to ascertain the dress code in a discreet manner before you start work, err on the side of smart. You can make the necessary correction the next day, but at first it is much better to arrive at work for a job as a janitor in a suit than to arrive in a janitor's jumpsuit for a job as a stockbroker. (See business attire on pages 86–88.)

Do not assume that your new employer will consider the same outfits that you wore to your last job as reasonable attire. On your first day, observe what everyone else is wearing and aim to create your own version of a similar outfit. Buy 'work' clothes if need be.

Even in workplaces where the dress code is casual, avoid miniskirts, shorts, flip-flops, transparent or fluorescent clothing, Hawaiian shirts, large amounts of jewellery and tops which expose cleavage or chest hair.

Desk appearance

Keep it tidy, even if this means setting aside an hour after work every week. You may know where everything is, but letting the papers and lost apples build up on your desk seems unprofessional to others.

By all means display photos, but stick to pictures of very close family rather than your family tree plus pets. Keep frames to a minimum. One group photo looks considerably tidier than five individual photos. Signed topless photos of your favourite page 3 model are not winsome, even if you work at *The Sun*. If you want a plant, make it a small one and make it only the one. Others can find jungles in the corner of the office distracting.

Clear out your desk drawers once every three months at an absolute minimum. You will undoubtedly find that missing gym sock causing the strange smell.

Eating at your desk

Does anyone really manage to continue working while they eat? Probably not. Although many companies consider a working lunch to be part of the standard day, eating over your desk is likely to be a messy and unhygienic business. Most offices have a canteen or eating area, and even if the trip is very brief, you should use it. In addition, the break from your desk has been proven to improve productivity.

Hot food should never be consumed at your desk in an open-plan office. The aromas of hot food tend to linger unpleasantly and the enticing scent of chicken masala will seem vomit inducing by 4.00 p.m. in a hot office. If absolutely necessary, cold, non-pungent, non-crumbly food can be eaten at the desk but only if done very carefully, using a napkin draped over your keyboard.

Open-plan offices

There is no need to shout on the phone. Neither is there a need to shout across the office – use the internal telephone numbers instead. Be mindful of allergies and strong odours. Go easy on perfumes and colognes so that only you or someone hugging you can smell them. If a colleague on a neighbouring desk has an allergy to peanuts/potted plant/perfume, then the owner of the allergy irritant should remove the offending article. If, however, a colleague on a neighbouring desk is allergic to dog hair brought in on your clothing, it is for them to take anti-allergy tablets or to ask to be moved. It is not your duty to give up your treasured pet poodle.

Telephone manners (as distinct from mobile phone manners)

Here are some basic rules for using the work telephone:

▶ *Answer the phone either as the company instructs you or with your name.*

▶ *Only put people on hold if you absolutely must. Despite it being a musical masterpiece of its time, it is unacceptable to force someone to listen to 'Greensleeves' (or whatever other awful tune is set as hold music) for longer than two minutes unless you are choking. If possible, give an estimated time that the caller will be on hold for and offer to call them back. Always warn the person on the other end of the line if you are about to put them on hold, and ask whether they would prefer to call back later.*

▶ *Don't answer calls in meetings and then say snottily, 'I'm in a meeting'. Let the answerphone get it or be prepared to answer urgent questions and explain your abruptness with civility.*

▶ *Warn someone if they are on speakerphone at the start of the conversation. If more than one person is speaking into the speakerphone, let each person introduce themselves in order for the call recipient to be able to identify the voices.*

▶ *If you work in an open-plan office, do not take calls on speakerphone if you are the only person speaking. It will be unnecessarily distracting for everyone else. If you want your hands free, use a headset, even if it does make you look a bit of an idiot.*

▶ *Likewise, when checking voicemails, do not use the speakerphone function. This is as much for your benefit as for those around you. After all, you won't know who has called until you listen to the messages.*

▶ *Make calls yourself. If you have an assistant, don't ask him or her to dial a number then put the person receiving the call on hold until they transfer the call to you. Just dial the number yourself.*

LEAVING MESSAGES

Start with saying who you are, the date and the time. Explain the purpose of your call in as few words as possible, conveying the level of urgency and what you require in response.

Whether you are a CEO or a secretary, return calls promptly. This is not a game of playing hard to get – in the working world returning calls as soon as possible is a mark of respect.

If you intend to be out of the office during working hours, set up a call divert to your mobile if necessary and an out of office auto-reply on your emails so that others are not perplexed by your lack of reply. As standard, change your voicemail message if you intend to be out of the office for a day or more. In the voicemail message and out of office auto-reply, give a date when you intend to return and attend to messages and an alternative contact number for someone in the company who may be able to deal with the request if it is urgent.

Introductions

When making introductions for business purposes, always introduce those lower down in the hierarchy to those higher up, regardless of age or gender. That is, if A is lower down the work pecking order than B, A's name goes second in a phrase, for example, 'B, it is my pleasure to introduce A'. Shake hands. In Britain, only air kiss if you socialize with the person at non-work-related occasions.

For networking events see page 7.

Use of computers

At work, use the computers available for work. Many employers expect a light personal use of work computers but there are particular websites which are sure to raise hairs on the back of any employer's neck, and with good reason. These include:

- ▶ *job/recruitment company websites*
- ▶ *rival company job application pages*
- ▶ *pornography sites*
- ▶ *music download sites, particularly pirated music.*

In addition to these, excessive use of other websites, for example, social networking sites such as Facebook, Bebo or MySpace, popular sites such as YouTube and eBay or personal webmail sites are bound to be considered by your employers as a distracting use of work resources.

Don't think you can get away with any of the above by having sharp reflexes and a trigger finger hovering on the close button. Many employers have networked 'alarms' set to some of the most popular sites or ones which cause them the most concern in order to monitor your use of them, and keep a meticulous record of time spent on these sites.

Emailing

For the etiquette of structuring work emails, see pages 95–98. In addition, however, be aware that your employer is likely to tolerate a light to moderate flow of personal emailing from your work account but heavy usage (receipt and reply taking more than five minutes per hour) is likely to affect your work and is thus considered bad working manners by your employer. It is better to use a personal email account for all personal emails, but if you are using a work account, never say anything bad or embarrassing about your company or employers within those emails, as they may be forwarded on with your work logo proudly displayed at the bottom.

Always prioritize work emailing. If you can't keep up with the flow of personal emailing, wait until after work hours to reply or call the friend in question to have a conversation during a break.

Dealing with your boss

Be polite and respectful. Some bosses may be jovial and have a cracking sense of humour. If so, joke with them and banter as though they are a friend. Indeed, some bosses are friends. However, some aren't, so no matter how funny their vicar-met-a-penguin jokes, be mindful of the difference and remember that sometimes even the best of friends occasionally fall out for good.

If you must go to your boss with problems, go with a list of potential solutions also.

Complaining to your boss about others

Always try to fix the complaint yourself by emailing the person at fault, explaining why you find their behaviour troubling and that you would like them to stop. If the problem persists, complain to your immediate boss.

Complaining to any higher power about the inappropriate behaviour of others does seem a little like tittle-tattling, no matter how you sugar-coat it. However, if there is a problem at work that is affecting your work, even if that problem is merely the inappropriate behaviour of others, you should tell your immediate boss. The easiest way to do this is to send an email saying that you have a problem at work that you would like to discuss and suggest a time and place where you can talk privately. At the meeting, tell your boss what it is that is concerning you and explain how it is affecting your work.

If your boss is the one causing you trouble, email them explaining the problem and how it is affecting your work. If the problem persists, email again. If the problem still persists, complain to their equal (if one exists) via email asking for their assistance in communicating with your boss. If the problem still doesn't improve, or the equal does not wish to become involved, then email your boss's boss, explaining the problem clearly and concisely.

Insight

When complaining about your boss to others at work, remember that gossip tends to travel fast. Be careful what you say. Hold your tongue.

If it is a serious problem such as a health and safety issue or harassment (sexual or racial for example), email once to complain to the person in question and after that complain to your immediate boss or your employer's immediate boss.

When complaining, save copies of all correspondence.

Negotiating a pay rise

Few companies give unrequested rises past a reflection of inflation, so if you want one, you will need to ask and be persuasive. Organize a meeting where you will have your boss's undivided attention. Go armed with reasons why you should be given the rise you are requesting. Good reasons are your worth to the company or having discovered that an equally qualified person doing the same job within the company is on a higher pay scale. Bad reasons are personal problems.

Never say that you can earn more elsewhere unless you actually do have a better paid job lined up that you wouldn't mind taking. Your boss may choose to call your bluff, shake your hand and wish you luck in your future career.

If you are not granted a pay rise which you feel was deserved on the basis of one of the 'good' reasons outlined above, decide whether you want to stay with the company. If you do, work harder and try again in three months, addressing any points your boss has highlighted for not granting you the rise. If the rise is still not granted, again consider leaving.

Quitting

If you have decided to leave, call a meeting with your boss.

Think through the reasons why you want to quit your job and decide whether they are potentially surmountable. For example, an accountant may want to quit because they do not like the company coffee and wants a bigger pay packet. These are potentially surmountable problems. However, a sudden fear of numbers after a traumatic experience with a calculator, for example, is insurmountable. Depending on which category your objections fall into, approach the meeting as a discussion (where you do not threaten to leave, you simply choose to at the end if the problems cannot be overcome), or a notification of the start of your notice period. If the latter, do not state your reasons for leaving unless you are asked (and you inevitably will be).

It is better to explain your reasons for departing face to face rather than simply submitting a letter of resignation, but take a written notice of departure to the meeting. This note should take the form of a formal letter to the company, starting 'Dear sirs', rather than being specifically addressed to your boss. The body of the text should contain the date, a clarification that this is notice of your resignation and the expected date of your last day. Give an appropriate (or contract stipulated) amount of notice to enable your employer to start the search for your replacement.

In addition, your letter should also express some regret about leaving if you want a good reference (don't go over the top, otherwise the company will think you have acquired a taste for sarcasm – one line will suffice). The letter should not outline your reasons for quitting, these should only be expressed face to face.

Never quit in a temper. If you change your mind once your emotions have settled you may not be able to change your unemployed job status.

If made redundant or fired

Keep your temper and ask for clear reasons behind the company's decision and an outline of any compensation package due. Ask for every detail in writing in case you decide to take legal action. If you are being fired for an event which is patently not your fault, say so, but say it calmly and clearly.

Insight
Even if your powers of persuasion are strong, it is unlikely that the decision can be reversed with ease. Set out your point of view calmly and clearly in strictly professional terms verbally and in writing.

Out-of-office socializing

Although a few people in your office may be counted among your true friends, not all will be. As the drink flows, tongues loosen and suddenly you're telling everyone how you once had a threesome with your boss and the photocopier guy in the mailroom. The problems faced the next morning need no explaining, particularly when it transpired during the course of the evening that Eileen from accounts, who controls your expense account, was seeing the photocopier guy when the aforementioned mailroom incident took place.

In drunken exploits with friends, dancing on a table in McDonald's will raise you to legend status. On a work night out, it will render you a liability at social events with clients. Don't see open bars at work events as an 'all you can drink' challenge. Aim to finish the night able to walk in a straight line and certainly without being sick. Guard secrets as you would a newborn baby in a riot.

If you can, avoid talking about work at all. Steer topics of conversation to hobbies, families, friends, etc. Ask lots of questions. They are much safer and will likely earn you a reputation as an interesting person and a good conversationalist, a skill much valued in the workplace.

Gossip

Although days tend to drag without it, only gossip about others if you would be willing for them to know your darkest secrets and discuss them around a watercooler. In social environments, gossip is often not nice, but in the work environment it can be harmful to a colleague's career.

Giving to work collections

Work collections may arise to celebrate events such as birthdays, weddings, a new baby and leaving presents. If your company is large (more than 40 people), there is no need to give to every donation. If you do not know the person, you do not need to open your wallet. If, however, you do know the person well enough to say hello to, give to the collection. Depending on your workplace, the standard amount of money each person gives for gifts will vary.

Try to gauge what is normal and do not let your donation drop below that figure.

Business travel abroad

Here are a few tips when travelling abroad on business:

▶ *Be aware of differences in introduction rituals. Some kiss, some handshake, others bow. Some cultures exchange business cards with much ceremony. Others say their company name before their own name. Learn how to execute the foreign introduction without embarrassment. Experts say it is important to research any sensitive cultural differences in greeting others as well as learning some key phrases in your host's language.*

▶ *Mind your personal space. The range of the area which is regarded as 'personal space' varies from country to country. In North America or Britain, 'social space' (people you chatter with) is between four and ten feet, 'personal space' (people you have a close, intimate or serious conversation with) is between two and four feet, and 'intimate space' (people with whom you are emotionally close, who may touch an arm or give a hug, for example) edges out to roughly a one foot radius. However, in Saudi Arabia or Russia, social space intrudes into British personal or intimate space, tending to make the British feel somewhat crowded. In other countries, the opposite is true – for example, the British intrude into Dutch personal space. If in doubt observe others, but certainly for business it is better to be seen as slightly standoffish than too immediately personal, so if in doubt stand back a little further than you are accustomed and wait for the other party to step forward if they feel more comfortable closer.*

▶ *If you do business regularly with companies in a foreign-language speaking country, consider having two versions of your business card, one in your language and one in another*

country's language, or a business card with a translation of
your details on the reverse.

▶ Learn key phrases and appropriate forms of address and titles.
▶ Don't joke. Some countries consider serious business no
laughing matter, and others may simply have a language
where the humour does not translate.
▶ If in doubt, follow your host's lead. For example, at business
lunches, wait for your host to broach the subject of work.

Insight

When travelling with others on a business trip, allow others a
say in how much free time is spent together. While your idea
of a good time may be to hit the foreign bars together, your
travelling companion may prefer a few hours in the hotel
with a book. Try to come to some compromise, but do not
assume that travelling together means spending every minute
of the day together.

Business dining etiquette

In addition to the notes on table manners and dining etiquette in
Chapter 10, note the following when dining out on business:

▶ Don't cancel at the last minute unless absolutely necessary.
▶ Arrive on time. Always call ahead if you know you will be
late, but always wait at least 15 minutes before checking on
the whereabouts of your dining companion.
▶ Do not place mobile phones or briefcases on the table. Leave
them on a spare seat or on the floor.
▶ It is not necessary to adapt your eating style to suit another
culture, unless the eating style requires different tools. For
example, British and American styles of eating are acceptable
in each other's countries because they both involve a knife
and fork, but eating roast beef and Yorkshire pudding with
chopsticks would be unacceptable.

- ▶ *Don't order the most expensive item.*
- ▶ *Avoid food that requires concentration.*

Insight

If it is absolutely necessary to cancel at the last minute, make sure that your dining partner gets the message. Remember that not everyone has a BlackBerry. If you can't speak to them directly, send an email with a read receipt attached as well as a voicemail. Call their office and ask someone there if there is a better alternative way of reaching them.

10 THINGS TO REMEMBER

1   *Welcome newcomers by offering to go out for a group lunch within the first fortnight.*

2   *Steer away from office romance, but if you must get involved, do so with caution and remain strictly professional at work.*

3   *Use your work email address for work email. Keep a personal email account active for personal emails. Prioritize work emails over chit-chat with friends.*

4   *Try to resolve problems with colleagues directly before involving your boss.*

5   *Don't ask others what they are paid. If they want you to know, they'll mention it themselves.*

6   *Take care of your personal appearance and hygiene.*

7   *Keep your desk tidy and regularly cleaned out.*

8   *Don't have conversations across open-plan office. You will disturb others. Either walk over or use the phone.*

9   *Don't take calls on speakerphones in open-plan offices if you are the only person speaking.*

10 *When quitting, be brave and do it face to face, but have a resignation letter ready to hand over.*

5

House sharing

In this chapter you will learn how to:
- *choose your flatmates/housemates*
- *live harmoniously*
- *deal with your landlord/tenants*
- *have guests*
- *move out.*

As property prices are still sky-high, more people than ever before share flats and houses. Some see the advantages of company on dull nights in front of the television while others simply embrace the reduced rent. However, whatever the underlying reason for the flat share, familiarity often breeds contempt when housemates do not show due care and consideration for each other.

Below is a selection of common house or flat sharing difficulties and suggestions on how to overcome them. In general, though, avoid problems by solving them rather than merely complaining about them. Discuss issues rather than shouting or brooding. Often people are not aware that their habits are annoying. It is possible that their toenail clipping in front of *The Simpsons* has never raised an eyebrow before.

Many behave around flatmates as they do around family, assuming that closeness implies unconditional forgiveness for bad behaviour. Even if this is the case, it is simply nicer to be reliable, thoughtful and considerate. Try to do more than expected and be understanding of pressures on sharers such as exams or job interviews, then maybe when you are on the brink of a nervous breakdown and forget to wash your cereal bowl, your housemates may be more inclined to give it a quick rinse without a soap opera-style drama.

Renting

Landlords and tenants have a tendency to regard each other with barely disguised hatred, for no real reason at all.

LANDLORDS

When showing potential tenants around an accommodation to let, remember that they are choosing the property and you are choosing the tenants. It is unlikely that the majority of tenants will magically transform into rave-inciting hell raisers the moment your back is turned. Some level of trust, as well as a deposit, will be needed to ensure the let continues smoothly. If the bland accountants that you have let the property to do indeed decide to stencil skulls and crossbones on the walls and burn cigarette-shaped holes in the carpet, take the money required for the repair work out of their deposits.

Remember that it is illegal to enter a let property without the permission of the tenants or unless a scheduled inspection of the property has been written into the lease contract.

Act promptly on requests from your tenants to fix items (like a dodgy dishwasher) or systems (like the plumbing) incorporated into the tenancy agreement. Tenants treat landlords who treat them well with respect, and are also likely to want to extend their stay.

The deposit which you received at the start of the let is not your money. You have it as a bond of good behaviour from your tenants. Do not invent reasons for keeping it at the end of the let (such as claiming money for the repainting of a wall because you notice a scratch at the top of a ten-foot ceiling after the house was let to a family of midgets). Don't be a walkover but be fair.

TENANTS

Remember that you are in someone else's property. Although you have paid for this privilege, this means that a certain level of respect for the items of the house is called for. If an item belonging to the house is broken by accident rather than by normal wear and tear, replace it with an item of similar function and value and tell the landlord what you have done immediately. Do not wait to confess your mishap at the end of your tenancy. Do not paint the walls or make any irreversible changes to the house without the prior consent of the landlord. If consent is denied, no means no.

If there is a problem with an item or system within the house covered by the tenancy agreement, tell your landlord promptly (the landlord is not clairvoyant). Also put it in writing. Be persistent. You are not nagging. It is a tenant's right to what was promised and paid for.

If you have been a polite tenant, have always paid your rent on time and have taken care of the place you are renting, you may ask the landlord to reconsider a rent increase on the grounds that the landlord's investment is in good hands and thus general maintenance on the property is likely to be reduced. However, before doing so, check rental prices of similar houses in the area to ensure that the rent you were paying previously was not unusually low.

Sort out all bills before you leave the house and leave a record of all bills paid (making a copy for yourself) for the landlord's peace of mind. Turn in all keys promptly.

Choosing flatmates

Those who flatshare will be moving in with either friends or strangers. Each has its share of advantages and disadvantages.

Many a friendship has been lost as a result of living together and strangers are an unknown that could land you sharing a bathroom and kitchen with a stamp collecting rabbit fur obsessive.

When choosing flatmates who are friends, consider not just how well you mooch along socially, but also what type of person they would be to live with. Be honest to them about how you live. Tell them if you insist upon nudist Thursdays or have just started learning to play the violin. Give them an idea of whether you are messy or obsessively compulsively neat or somewhere in between. Be painfully honest and upfront about what your friend(s) can expect should they move in with you. That way, even if the arrangement is not satisfactory, all parties will leave it without feeling duped.

If you are moving in with strangers, honesty about living habits is also required, but the approach to this may seem in breach of other etiquette norm. For example, elsewhere in this book it is recommended that discussion about money is rude, that it is poor etiquette to ask outright about cleanliness of living or immediately about relationship status. In this scenario, these personal questions should be asked as the answers are critical to choosing a housemate. However, in order not to seem rude, the meeting and choosing process should be far more formal, as set out below.

Before meeting potential flatmates who are not (yet) friends, first have a screening phone call in order to ensure you are not wasting either your or their time. Send a text or email to arrange a suitable time at which you can call the other person for a chat. Ask a lot of questions, from how old the person is, to what they do for a living, to what their taste in music is like and what football team they support and whether they have any pets. If you do not think that the person is suitable, tell them immediately, claiming that you just don't think your living habits would be compatible. If you believe that the person may be suitable, arrange a time and date at which you can meet in person (this may also include a flat viewing if the flat already exists or has been chosen). On this phone call, you may not ask about the person's appearance unless it is necessary to identify them; most have a warped view of what they look like anyway.

For the face-to-face meeting, prepare to ask and answer questions. Both sides should consider and ask permission to take a friend along for a second opinion or for safety reasons. Make sure that the room and flat you are letting is clean and tidy. As this may be the last time you meet before the decision on both sides is made, it is important that potential housemates are given realistic expectations of what to expect if they do move in. Take notes and both sides should be given a deadline for making a decision.

Among other similar questions, it is not rude to ask about the following:

▶ *whether the potential housemate smokes, uses drugs and to what extent drinks*
▶ *how much the rent and bills are and what is included in each figure*
▶ *eating habits*
▶ *daily routines*
▶ *food sharing*
▶ *whether guests are permitted to stay and whether there are any house rules about this issue*
▶ *what the neighbourhood is like*
▶ *extreme political or religious positions*
▶ *lifestyle oddities*
▶ *house rules*
▶ *occupation, employer and the person's age*
▶ *where they are living now and why they are moving*
▶ *availability of references from previous housemates*
▶ *existence of medical issues that could affect the sharing*
▶ *spare time activities and interests, music and television programme preferences*
▶ *relationship status and how often partners stay*
▶ *likely frequency of friends visiting and what these friends enjoy*

- *affordability of rent (it is okay to ask whether the potential tenant will be on a regular wage; it is not okay to ask how much that wage is)*
- *whether they have any pets*
- *sexual orientation if it something which may bother the existing flatmates. Homophobia is not nice but it exists and if it is going to create a hostile living environment for the new housemate, it is a relevant question.*

Most questions are permissible if asked in the right way and are relevant to whether you will be able to live harmoniously with the potential housemate. However, there are some questions you may not ask – these normally fall into the category of personal curiosity and will give no real insight to whether the housemate would be suitable. Two examples of such questions are:

- *why a potential housemate is single*
- *what the potential housemate's parents do, or any sort of query regarding class background.*

In addition, you will just have to wait until the potential housemate moves in to find out:

- *whether they have loud sex, or sexual fetishes of any other sort (you'll just have to buy earplugs)*
- *whether a female suffers from bad PMT (she might not admit to it anyway).*

You may request a second face-to-face meeting if either of you wish.

Do not move into a house with someone who you are initially sexually attracted to. If this is the motive for your wanting to live together, ask them out on a date instead.

Inform unsuccessful applicants as soon as possible. For those where the living arrangement seems suitable, set a firm date for the person to move in and have a clean room and key waiting.

Remember that upon moving in, the newcomer becomes a member of the household with equal rights. If there are disagreements after this point, just because they are the most recent entrant to the living arrangement does not make their opinion invalid or their complaint less serious.

Day-to-day issues

CLEANING

The sharing of cleaning duties is the most likely irritant between otherwise tolerant and well-behaved flatmates. There really is no excuse for not having done your washing up. If you don't have time to wash up, you shouldn't have time to eat. If you forget to do the dishes, do them the moment you set foot back into the house. For some, having to wash an item of kitchenware before using it themselves is the psychological equivalent of having to clean the whole house before eating, even if it was just a fork. It is insulting to other flatmates to assume that your time is more precious than theirs, which is the underlying implication of not having done this simple chore. If you have a spare five minutes, and you are washing your own dishes, finish off a few of your flatmates'. The gesture will be appreciated and may even be reciprocated later on.

Work out a rota, even if it is an informal one, for larger cleaning duties such as vacuuming, cleaning the oven and cleaning the bathroom.

There will, undoubtedly, be one flatmate who is tidier than the others, who wants the floor vacuumed every day, skirting boards dusted at the weekends and the curtains hung perfectly straight. This person is likely to be irked by a lot of the behaviour of his/her flatmates, but will not understand why their nagging is a source of irritation. Those tidy beings should remember that they have an entitlement to hygienic, habitable surroundings but little else. Only nag if washing up has not been done after 24 hours, not two. If you want the skirting boards dusted every weekend, do it yourself. Talk to your flatmates about those aspects of living which concern you most and hopefully they will oblige in making the situation more comfortable for you all. If standards do not improve, suggest a cleaner. If this suggestion is unacceptable to the flatmates, move out and consider living on your own.

If a flatmate has left their washing in the washing machine and you need to use it, take the washing out and, if you have the time, hang it up to dry. If not, leave it in a washing basket or on a clean table and leave a note for your flatmate informing them of the whereabouts of their clothing. Never leave it on the floor and never throw all the items in the tumble dryer and turn it on to high unless you have scrutinized every piece for 'do not tumble dry' warnings. Your kind act may shrink every favourite item of your flatmate's carefully put together fluorescent vintage 80s wardrobe.

As well as doing the dishes, keep common areas tidy so that everyone can invite people home at the last minute.

FOOD

Unless you share all the food in the house and the bill, do not eat anything you have not purchased yourself. Eating your flatmate's food is theft. If an uncontrollable kleptomanic urge to raid the fridge comes upon you in the small hours of the morning, leave a note itemizing your pillaging, promising to replace it. Return the food immediately the next day, even if this means making an unplanned trip to the shops while you are hungover and queasy.

Do not hog the fridge or cupboards. Bizarrely, flat shares always come with a fridge that is far too small. Pack items sensibly and do half-weekly rather than weekly shops if necessary. Also, consider sharing items that you all use, for example milk.

Be particularly careful when you are storing meat or smelly foods. Pack in an extra container or wrapping to ensure that meat doesn't leak or a strong smell does not contaminate the other items in the fridge. Throw out your own and others' stale items promptly.

When cooking, shut the kitchen door to prevent the smell from permeating the whole house. Nobody enjoys the smell of salmon on the living room cushions.

Never lose your temper over milk or bread. Fifty pence every week simply isn't worth the loss of friendship or high blood pressure.

PRIVACY

One of the most difficult aspects of house sharing is the lack of privacy. Communal areas are indeed communal but try to avoid leaving your belongings scattered about. Bedrooms are places of absolute privacy. Whether the flatmate is in or out of the house, their bedroom is a place which should only be entered when invited, even to perform favours such as delivering folded washing. Leave the washing on a table in the living room or outside their door. Never borrow anything from a bedroom without either asking first or being invited to do so. Never assume that permission to do so once covers you for any other time you want to borrow something from the sacred zone.

Never think it is acceptable to use a flatmate's room as a guest bedroom unless they have offered it up for that purpose themselves. By all means drop subtle hints in order to give your flatmate the opportunity to suggest, but don't ask outright as it should not be a favour they feel pressured into granting.

Give each other space to be alone from time to time. Go to the houses of your friends sometimes instead of inviting your friends over to yours.

HOUSE PHONE USE AND MESSAGES

Don't hog the phone and do offer to pay extra if:

▶ *you have been calling foreign countries*
▶ *you have been calling premium line numbers regularly*
▶ *your phone use clearly outweighs your flatmates'.*

If you have a dial-up connection, be mindful that your internet use may be preventing someone else from using the phone or internet. Check with others that this is not the case.

If there is a house phone, messages taken for other flatmates should be written down clearly with a time and date and left in an agreed place.

Personal hygiene and general courtesy

Keep yourself and your room clean. Watching *Neighbours* with a flatmate who did not shower after the gym is not a pleasant experience. Although your bedroom is private, having a room smelling of weeks' worth of body odour and unwashed sheets and underwear is unpleasant for flatmates knocking on your door.

HAVING FRIENDS TO STAY

Where possible, give warning to your flatmates and ask permission if you plan for a friend or relative to stay the night. This is a must when the arrangement is for more than one night, even if the guest is sleeping in your room. Nobody likes to walk into the living room of their own house, half-dressed, ready to watch Saturday morning television, only to find a snoring beauty on the sofa. If the arrangement is an impromptu one, leave a note on the living room door to warn of what lies inside.

Insight
Gently let friends know of any house rules immediately upon arrival.

If you are the unexpected snoring beauty, check with all the awake flatmates that they do not need to urgently use the bathroom before you take a shower. Use only the showering products belonging to the friend who invited you to stay. In addition, before you leave the area, buy a bunch of flowers or a six-pack of beer for the flatmates as a thank you for the use of their sofa and an apology for any inconvenience caused.

Flatmates should not assume that it is fine to have friends to stay all the time on the couch. About once a week is acceptable; more frequently is abusing your flatmates' kindness.

Insight

If you are staying at a friend's house, never bring back a friend or lover of your own.

If you arrive at your flat with company late at night, remember that your flatmates may be asleep. Ask your guest to keep their voice low and do the same yourself. Play music or watch television only at a level which will not disturb the sleep of others in the house. If you do wake one of your flatmates, apologize profusely and turn the offending item off entirely.

Insight

If you are having a friend to stay, they are your responsibility. It falls to you to do their washing up if they forget, and if they don't buy your flatmates a present as a thank you, you should.

BATHROOM USE

Don't be a bathroom hog. Allocate times for bathroom use in the morning rush. Wash the bath or shower down after use. Leave no trace of saliva, toothpaste, shaving foam or hair in the sink. If there is a lingering smell after you have used the toilet, use air freshener or strike a match to remove the odour.

Open the window after a steamy shower and never take a long bath without first asking your flatmates whether they will need the bathroom in the next hour. Do not borrow the shampoo, hair conditioner or any other showering product belonging to your flatmates without specifically asking each time. Permission to do so once should not be taken as a general granting of permission for all times. This is as much petty theft (and not so petty if their face cream, etc. is Clarins, Decléor, Christian Dior, Chanel or any other brand imported and unnecessarily expensive) as stealing food from the fridge or jewellery from a flatmate's room.

Only ever use your own bath towel. Use a communal towel to dry your hands or face, not a flatmate's bath towel. Equally, if you are daft enough to leave your towel in the bathroom, expect that at some point someone who isn't you will use it.

HAVING LOVERS TO STAY

Remember that your flatmates have chosen to live with you, not you and the current love of your life. Don't monopolize the sofa or remote control with your partner. Your friends, particularly the single ones, will be more resentful of the extra body in the house if that body is the reason they cannot watch the *Hollyoaks* omnibus.

> **Insight**
> Don't let your lover walk around the house that you share with others naked or in just their underwear.

There should be no displays of affection or anger between the two of you. The former is sick making and the latter disruptive. Make sure that you stay at your partner's house as much as he/she stays at yours. This way there can be no argument about the extra use of electricity/milk/loo roll in either of your flats. If your relationship somehow unravels such that your partner stays at your shared house for more than half the week, contribute a little more than other flatmates for house bills. If your partner is spending close to every night at your house, consider moving out of the shared house and in with your partner. Chances are that the house you are in is not equipped to deal with the extra body.

> **Insight**
> Have sex as quietly as you can. The activity should not be a compulsory aural experience for those you share the house with.

If you do overhear someone having sex when you were clearly not meant to, turn some music or the TV on or leave the house. Don't mention it to your flatmate.

BREAKAGES

Treat the belongings of your flatmates with even more care than you would your own, but if something does get broken, don't try to cover it up. Buy a replacement of equal or increased value and apologize. If the item was of sentimental value, buy a replacement as well as an extra personal gift. Never suggest that an item of such personal or monetary value should have been kept somewhere safer.

Throwing parties

Always invite the neighbours. They are unlikely to attend, and so unlikely complain about noise levels if they are 'guests' letting you down by not attending themselves. Be mindful of small children living next door. Give parents a time when the music will be turned off and the party stopped or moved to a different venue.

If sending one flatmate to do the party shopping, decide on a detailed shopping list before that person sets off. There is little more soul destroying (or foolish) in a student house, than sending your flatmate (whose parents happen to own a Swiss bank) out on this mission and discovering that the cheapo party you were planning on throwing has now cost you £200 a piece, with the flatmate in question having purchased nothing more than an ice sculpture, champagne and canapés. However, if you have not discussed the shopping list or budget before your flatmate sets out, you have no right to complain about whatever they bring back.

Accept strangers into your house. If you are sensible you will have hidden all the valuables before the party started, and the gatecrashers are likely to be friends of friends of your flatmates.

Split the bill by a rough proportion of the guests you have invited. If every member of the house has invited a roughly equal number of guests, split the bill equally.

THROWING DINNER PARTIES

If you are living in a shared flat, do not host a dinner party without inviting your flatmates, as the event will take over at least one communal space for the duration of the event. Flatmates are under no obligation to attend, but if they don't, they should make themselves scarce that evening.

Moving out

If you intend to move out, give your flatmates at least one month's notice – more, if possible, as they are likely to need to find a replacement to fill your room and pay your share of the rent. If possible, suggest people who you know are looking for a place to stay, but do not actually arrange a replacement without your flatmates' permission.

Before you leave, clean your room thoroughly. Also make sure that any mess you have created throughout your stay in the rest of the house is tidied before you depart. It is a nice gesture to leave flowers, chocolates or some other thoughtful gift as a present to the flatmates you have left behind, together with a note saying that you will miss them all. Miraculously, soon after you leave, they will forget all about your terrible cleaning skills and remember only the beautiful bouquet/chocolates/keg of beer that remained.

If you are all leaving the flat as a group, divide up the intensive cleaning. Cleaning a flat ready for inspection is a big task and swift departures without having spent substantial time in rubber gloves and smelling of bleach will not endear you to your ex-flatmates.

Miscellaneous

Showing consideration for your neighbours largely consists of keeping your voice and your music down low. They may have children or jobs with early morning starts and will not appreciate your karaoke singing at three in the morning. Also, keep piano/trombone/violin practice at a civilized hour (remember that Sunday mornings are not considered civilized for some) and in short bursts.

Pay maintenance costs on buildings on time and try to contribute to residents' meetings. Don't leave rubbish in communal hallways and follow the laws of the building/complex you are in.

Living as a couple

Continue to say please, thank you and sorry. Do nice things for each other. Remember that this person you are sharing your house with is also your best friend and live with them as such. If you are cooking meals for each other, let each other know when you will not be home for supper before the other person starts cooking. Wash down the bath to remove stray hairs. Offer to make each other cups of tea. Love does not mean never having to say that you are sorry.

Cheating on your partner is poor etiquette to start off with, but having sex in a bed you share with your partner is unforgivably grimy behaviour.

In flats or houses shared by couples, less emphasis will be placed on the individual and more on being together: sharing food, one cooking and the other washing up, etc. A natural division of chores may emerge but split them equally if both partners are working. In particular, try to remember that whoever has done the cooking should not also be lumbered with the washing up and eating the last Rolo or mini quiche is not nice if they are your partner's favourite.

10 THINGS TO REMEMBER

1   *Be honest about your living habits and the house when asking others to move in with you.*

2   *Share the cleaning. Draw up a rota if necessary.*

3   *Keep common areas tidy so that flatmates can invite others home at short notice.*

4   *Try to be tolerant if others do not share your high standards of tidiness and do a little extra if you prefer things a certain way.*

5   *Avoid arguments by talking calmly about problems.*

6   *Don't take food that is not yours. If you must, check with your flatmate first that this is acceptable and replace it as soon as possible even if it inconveniences you to do so.*

7   *Don't have guests to stay without asking the permission of flatmates. For lovers, ensure that you stay in your lover's house as much as your lover stays in yours and don't inconvenience others while your lover is staying.*

8   *Bedrooms are areas of privacy. Do not enter a flatmate's room without being invited, do not use it as a guest bedroom and do not borrow items from it.*

9   *Replace broken items belonging to your flatmates immediately.*

10   *When moving out, give sufficient notice and clean up all your mess before departing.*

6

Being a good host and guest

In this chapter you will learn how to:
- *hold a party or dinner party*
- *cope with difficult guests*
- *attend a party or dinner party without causing offence*
- *make yourself an unobtrusive guest.*

Hosting a dinner party

WHAT TO COOK

Cook a dish that you believe your guests will want to eat, not one that showcases your own exotic culinary tastes and skills. Also, cook something that you are practised at – now is not the time to try a soufflé or some unpronounceable French dish that you have never whipped up before. If disaster strikes, be prepared with the telephone number of a good takeaway that delivers. Prepare dishes so there is minimal fuss between courses.

Always cook more than you think will be needed in case of unexpected guests or extra large appetites. It is far better in terms of etiquette to have a lot go to waste than to leave your guests hungry at the end of a meal.

ALLERGIES AND SPECIAL DIETARY REQUIREMENTS

If one of your guests rings you beforehand to warn you of an allergy, change what you had planned to serve to all in order to avoid using that ingredient, rather than making a special dish for that one guest. Thus, the allergy sufferer is not made to feel that they have inconvenienced you in any way.

It is advisable when shopping for your dinner party to pick up extra items that you would like to eat throughout the coming week. Thus, if your guest forgets to warn you of their allergy, grit your teeth and take solace in the fact that you have a fridge full of food available to offer as an alternative. This is, however, going above and beyond the call of duty, and quite frankly if the allergy sufferer has not warned you of their problem, they should expect little else but bread and cheese.

Similarly, vegetarians should be accommodated by offering a meal for all which may be served complete with or without a meat component, thus satisfying the needs of both the omnivores and herbivores at the table. For example, serve a roast dinner with beef and nutloaf. Note, however, that vegetarians will not be fooled by your careful selection of vegetables from a pot which has been stewing together with the meat, and it is wise to remember that neither vegetarians nor vegans eat fish.

These days, as fad diets have become the norm, you may also be faced with the issue of Atkins dieters; dieters eating only at certain times of the day; dieters living only off the nutrients in special milkshakes; dieters who only want to eat vegetables; dieters who will only consume a certain sort of carbohydrate... Typically in etiquette, these people should not expect you to pander to their needs, but you should. If they do inform you of such a dietary 'requirement', as a good host you must endeavour to fulfil this need by altering your cooking plans to make their food part of the supper for all (for example, serve steak and mashed potatoes to the non-Atkins dieters and only steak to the Atkins dieter).

Call before you shop for ingredients to check with the fad dieter that what you are planning will be suitable as, with the complexity of some diets, it is easy to get it wrong. If, however, it is simply not possible to cater for this special dietary request by virtue of the time of day or type of food (for example, the milkshake diet), it is fair to express regret but suggest that the guest stops by just for drinks or make another arrangement to see the person.

SEATING PLANS

For groups of more than six people, give this some thought as it becomes impossible to speak to everyone throughout the meal. Boy–girl–boy–girl is the norm, but this is not a strict rule, and it is advisable to put come distance between those with strong opposing political or religious views or those who are likely to create conflict (for example ex-husbands and wives). Sit husbands and wives and lovers apart – they see each other every day, here they should be prepared to sing for their supper.

For formal dinner parties, the most important male guest sits next to the hostess and the most important female sits next to the host.

Hosting parties

Always over-invite to parties. For reasons ranging from food poisoning to the cancellation of baby sitters to the arising of a better offer (although this is very poor etiquette indeed), your planned number of guests may be depleted to a paltry few and it is your duty as a host to provide a certain number of guests to make the evening entertaining for those who do show up.

Provide an abundance of easy-to-serve alcohol as well as a good non-alcoholic alternative for designated drivers and teetotallers. Water is not a 'good' non-alcoholic alternative.

Always welcome gatecrashers to parties if they come with one of your invited guests, regardless of whether the party is being held at your house or an alternate venue. It is not, however, the done (or safe) thing to open your house freely to strangers on the street, although if you are feeling kindly you might not mind doing it in a bar, in which case it is a personal judgement call rather than a duty.

Special notes for the host

SMOKING

If you do not smoke in your house yourself, you do not have to tolerate others doing so. You should, however, in cold seasons be prepared for guests to smoke out of a window or to stand in an open doorway. At large parties in your own house, leave a sign on the front door asking guests kindly not to smoke indoors. If someone lights up inside, make no show of having noticed and wait for another guest to suggest they move outside.

DRUGS

As the host, it is your duty to make sure that everyone is having a good time. If you are high and at least one of your guests is sober, it is impossible to do this, so think carefully before indulging yourself.

If you notice your friends taking drugs and would prefer that they didn't in your house, tell them discreetly to stop. When inviting known drug users, phone before the event to indicate that you would prefer that they didn't on your property. If at any point your request for your guests to not take drugs is denied, you may ask them to leave.

ADVISING OF APPROPRIATE ATTIRE

If you want a specific sort of attire worn at your party or dinner party, specify it on the invitation. If your chosen dress code is something unconventional, a detailed description may be required.

When inviting guests to weekends away, let them know what sort of activities you have planned and if any of the activities or events state a dress code or will require clothing out of their everyday norm. This should allow your guests to make sensible decisions about what sort of clothing to bring – wellies and trainers for a weekend lambing on a farm, for example, and black tie for the evening farm ball.

DEALING WITH DRUNK GUESTS

If one of your guests hits the bottle a little hard, start circulating with some mineral water. If the guest is too inebriated to take the subtle hint, first rescue whoever has been trapped in conversation with him or her and then offer to call the swaying one a cab.

If an invited guest is ill owing to excessive alcohol consumption on your premises, you are under obligation to offer a spare room for the night or to provide litres of drinking water until the person is sober enough to travel home by cab or with another friend.

DEALING WITH AMOROUS ATTENTIONS

Hosts of parties are often objects of affection for the evening as they are likely to be, by definition, the most popular person in the room. Even if the party was thrown particularly with the purpose of meeting a special someone, it is not good form to spend the evening snogging in a corner like a thirteen-year-old as it will prevent you from circulating among other guests. Instead, if there is someone you would like to get your hands on, use the party as an opportunity to set the date for a more private situation.

If a guest makes an unwanted move on you, brush it off by laughing and make your excuses to use the restroom or to say hello to another guest. Tell one close friend of your predicament and ask for their assistance in removing you from one-on-one conversations with this guest as the night continues and more and more alcohol is consumed.

SAYING GOODBYE AND WALKING TO THE DOOR

For parties of more than ten guests, it is not necessary to walk each guest to the door to say goodbye as they leave.

Having friends to stay at your home

Having guests to stay at your home can be tiresome if you are not well prepared. Having a few extra bodies in the house may not seem like a big chore before your guests arrive, but no matter how long you have known them and how entertaining they are, you are likely to exhale a big sigh of relief when the time comes for them to depart.

BASICS

Lay down house rules with a smile as the guests arrive. For example, mention whether smoking is or is not allowed in the house; set out a quick bathroom usage agenda, adding if there is limited hot water; and if you plan to provide meals, say at what time. It is not necessary to give up your own bed at nights if you do not have a spare room, but you must warn guests before they arrive that they will be sleeping on the sofa or an airbed. Provide spare clean towels, a bedside light, magazines to keep an insomniac happy and a bottle of water and a fresh glass.

PROVIDING SOME ACTIVITIES

If your guests are staying for longer than a weekend, you need not offer to provide every meal. However, expect to cater for a minimum of breakfast and one other meal each day. Make it clear which meals your guests will be expected to fend for themselves. You should, however, offer a fully catered stay if the guests are in your company for just one weekend.

You have agreed to the staying of houseguests, not to be bound inextricably to them for the duration of a lengthy stay. Your guests may not know the area and its attractions well, so over a drink or meal when your guests first arrive, mention activities that may be suitable. Of course, if you want, suggest all going together, but it is sensible to arrange it so that at least one afternoon, morning or evening per three days is left so that the guests and host have an opportunity to get out of each other's sight, even if just for a couple of hours to give yourself a little breathing space. Use an excuse such as 'You really shouldn't miss it, but I've done it before and besides, it'll give me a chance to pop the washing on/call my sister/walk the dog.'

SAYING GOODBYE

If your guests are leaving at a sensible hour, that is, after 9.00 a.m. and before 11.00 p.m., it is kind to be on site to wave them goodbye at the doorstep, wish them a safe journey, provide a last-minute snack and tell them how lovely it has been to have them to stay (even if, in fact, your nightmare of a mother-in-law would have been less work).

However, if your guests are leaving at a ludicrously early or late hour, there is no need to be awake. Instead, bid your guests a fond farewell before you retire to bed, point them in the direction of the snack cupboard and fridge and give them a spare key to lock up after themselves and put through the letterbox.

Inviting friends on holiday

Think twice before inviting friends to stay for the weekend but think three times before inviting them on holiday. Inviting friends with whom to spend your free time may seem like a great idea at home but may not seem so great once you are away and feel the pressure of entertaining. It can be a pleasurable experience for all if ground rules are gently laid down during the planning stage; if it is made clear what will and will not be provided; if enough time spent apart is fitted in and if it is made clear at the outset how finances for the week will be managed.

Being a good guest

RESPONDING TO INVITATIONS

Reply promptly to invitations by the same medium that the invitation was received. Reply to written invitations within four days of receipt. Reply to email or text invitations by return. If you are unable to give a firm decision within these four days or by return, call the host to explain your predicament and ask whether a later decision can be made. If you forget to reply to an invitation, call to apologize and to ask whether the invitation still stands.

TIMING

For dinner parties, arrive on time. The host has likely spent hours slaving over a sumptuous meal, and being more than 15 minutes late may ruin it. If you are likely to be late, telephone ahead with as much notice as possible to warn your host and urge everyone to start without you. When you do arrive, apologize profusely to the host and take your place at the dining table quietly, trying not to draw attention to yourself.

Do not arrive early for dinner parties. Drive around the neighbourhood or refill your car with fuel to pass the time. Your host will likely be embroiled in a last-minute panic to get themselves, the house and the meal fit for company, and having to entertain a guest before the designated time will only add to their distress.

For parties, arrive any time from the exact time on the invite to an hour later. However, if you are going to be more than half an hour late, send your host a text to advise that you do still plan to attend.

For weekends away, if your journey has taken two hours or longer, you may arrive from an hour early to an hour late (provided that the host is not preparing a hot meal for your arrival). If your journey has taken less than two hours, arrive at the time specified (amuse yourself in the local village if necessary) or up to half an hour late. In either case, if you are going to be early, you must call to warn your host. If you are going to be more than 20 minutes late, it is also good manners to call in advance. It is always good manners to call as soon as you know that you will be early or late, but if your host is meeting you from a train station, airport or bus stop, this matter is even more pressing.

The dinner party/party guest

ALLERGIES OR SPECIAL DIETARY REQUIREMENTS/REQUESTS

If you want to attend a dinner party, call your host before you RSVP to let them know that you require a particular type of food. Try to be as flexible as you can – if you can break a diet for an evening without ruining the whole plan, for example, you should. Be understanding that your host may not be able to alter the menu, in which case express regret at missing their company and suggest coming for drinks after the meal has finished.

You may not call to simply state preferences. If you don't like blackberries and there is an apple and blackberry crumble for dessert, you are going to have to either stomach it or claim that you ate too much during the main meal.

SPEAKING TO THE LEFT AND THE RIGHT

When you are at supper, speak to the people on both sides of you. Start speaking to your dining neighbour on one side and give them your full attention. When the courses change, switch conversational partners. If you become engrossed in conversation with the first person, you should change conversational partners just before dessert. Be careful when switching partners, however, that there is no plan for men to switch seats between courses.

POLITE TOPICS OF CONVERSATION

Hobbies, pets (if you both have them), children (if you both have them), work, where you live and travel are all suitable topics of conversation (see Chapter 2 on The art of making conversation for more detail). Avoid politics, religion, money and medical conditions.

DEALING WITH OFFENSIVE COMMENTS

If someone in your company makes a politically incorrect comment in the form of racism, sexism or homophobia and you find this offensive, think before you lash out. Was this comment said in jest or in seriousness? If it was said in jest, let it slide – this person's sense of humour may not be to your own taste but he or she is simply trying to entertain rather than be offensive.

If, however, the comment was meant with no jest or humour attached, consider what is more important – the company of the people around you or your principles. Even if what they have said is grossly offensive, you may lose the good favour of your hosts and other guests by causing a scene or even making the atmosphere a little sticky. If you choose to stand up to the xenophobe, you get to keep your principles but prepare to leave at the earliest available opportunity and not to be invited back.

WHAT TO WEAR

If the invitation specifies a certain dress code, whether that be fancy dress, formal or casual, embrace it wholeheartedly as it helps the hosts create the atmosphere for the event. If it does not and you are unsure what to wear, call the host or another guest to check what would be considered acceptable attire for the evening. Use the form of invitation as a hint – an engraved invitation is likely to denote black tie whereas a text message is likely to encourage casual wear. Do not take a risk though – if there is any doubt in your mind, call the host.

SPILLAGE

If you spill a drink and the damage is only to an item of furniture, start mopping the table or furniture with your napkin immediately to avoid the soaking of every item. If the drink has spilt on another guest, hand them your napkin for use on themselves and leap up to find another absorbent item with which to attend to the table. Do not dab at the person you have soiled, in particular do not dab at their crotch. If you are the unfortunate recipient of a glass of red wine to the lap, deal with it with good grace. Excuse yourself, clean what you can, compose yourself and return to the table with a smile and calming comment such as 'I always hated these trousers anyway'. Lie if you must; this is not the time to reveal that your grandmother hand stitched the garment for you on her deathbed.

If the drink spills on yourself, attend to the table first and then excuse yourself to clean yourself up.

BRINGING EXTRA GUESTS

Never bring an uninvited guest to a dinner party. This includes spouses, children and pets. Do not ask your host for clarification – if their name was not mentioned through the invitation process, you must assume that they are not welcome. If you unexpectedly find yourself in a position that makes it difficult for you to attend without the company of an additional extra, your next move will be dependent upon how well you know the host. If the host can be counted as one of your ten best friends, you may call to explain the situation and ask whether it would be possible to bring them as well. If the host agrees, a large gift is in order, either upon arrival or sent after you leave, with particular thanks for their help in the tricky situation. If the host says that it is impossible, your additional extra will simply have to find a way to amuse him/herself for the evening.

If the host cannot be counted among your ten best friends, you cannot ask for a last-minute plus-one and your attendance at the supper is still mandatory. If you feel that time spent with the additional extra is necessary, explain the situation to the host, explaining why you must cancel at the last minute. The host may or may not then offer to accommodate the additional extra, but regardless of the outcome, your reason had better be good (and cannot fall under the category of 'better offers' – see below), for if the host believes it unjustified then you are unlikely to receive a second invitation.

For a party without a meal, if you want to bring additional guests, call the host to check that this is okay. At parties where food is not being served, he or she is unlikely to object, but if the host does have objections, accept their decision gracefully and without argument.

COMPLAINTS

Only draw the host's attention to problems or failings if the issue is health-threatening, for example undercooked chicken.

Insight

Present complaints as questions to the host rather than accusations. For example, say 'Do you think this chicken is undercooked?' rather than 'The chicken isn't cooked.' This puts the host in a position of control. They'll likely then check everyone's. If they disagree with you and you still think you are right, eat what you can and leave whatever you think will make you ill.

COMPLIMENTS

If a host has taken the time to organize an event that you have attended, your compliments are expected and should flow freely. However, after meals, you should compliment the whole meal as well as specific elements of it. Praising just specific parts suggests that the rest of the meal was a disaster.

BETTER OFFERS

At some point or another, we all accept one invitation (for example, tickets to a Take That tribute band) only to find out later that a better offer is available (for example, tickets to an actual Take That gig). No matter the disparity in value or company, never accept the better offer. The only exception to this is if the better offer is a momentous occasion in a friend's life, for example their engagement party or wedding, in which case apologies to your first commitment should be profuse and accompanied by an immediate rescheduling to see each other at your expense. Never accept a last-minute (within 24 hours) better offer.

EMBRACE THE WALLFLOWER

Help hosts by including those who seem shy or uninvolved in the fun. Hosts worry that not all of their guests are having a good time – helping to include everyone in conversation will alleviate this fear for the host.

Insight

Listen carefully when wallflowers speak and try to guide the subject of conversation to topics they find easy to talk about.

AMOROUS INTENTIONS

If you happen to find the soon-to-be love of your life at a party, you are allowed one discreet kiss, chatter, and a swapping of contact details. That is all. It is rude to snog openly and repetitively in public, to find a dark corner for a quick grope or to sneak into an empty bedroom for something further as this removes you from your duty as a guest to add to the general party atmosphere. Make sure that your amorous intentions are only directed towards the one party guest – at these events many people already know each other and your lack of devotion will be noted with distaste.

DEALING WITH UNWANTED ATTENTIONS

If another person at the party seems to want more than a chat and these attentions are unwelcome, include another person in conversation and then extricate yourself. If the attention giver does not get the message, smile politely and explain that you are just not looking for anyone at the moment.

PRYING EYES

Although as a host it would be foolish to leave medications for a private medical condition in easily accessible cabinets in the bathroom, as a guest it is a duty to ignore your curiosity about your hosts' personal lives. Don't snoop.

KNOWING WHEN THE PARTY IS OVER

The party is over when one or more of the hosts retires to bed; when the hosts can't stop yawning; when the bar is dry; or when everyone starts to put their coats on and move towards the door.

SAYING GOODBYES

At parties, if your host is occupied with another guest and there are more than 20 people in the room, it is acceptable to wave a goodbye or even leave without having said goodbye (however, if you do it is essential that you send a thank-you message). There is no need to say goodbye individually to each person you have spoken to, but if you are a man and there are more than four women in the room, try not to kiss the first one unless you want to be there for another half an hour kissing them all.

The weekend guest

No matter how well-meaning the invitation, where possible stay at a nearby guest house or hotel instead of at the home of your hosts. Stress on both parties is thus reduced, and besides, by the time you pay for a broken item and take the hosts on a day trip and out for supper, the cost to your pocket is virtually the same.

PETS AND EXTRA FAMILY MEMBERS

Pets and additional family members are not welcome if the invitation does not include them. It is difficult enough entertaining one person or a couple for a weekend without their entourage of dogs, cats, hamsters, budgies and infants. If you are at pains to leave these, check into a guest house that welcomes these sorts of creatures and visit your friends during the day.

ADAPTING TO A HOST'S LIFESTYLE

People have different living habits. Some like to sleep late, others like to rise early. Some like to shower, others like to bath. Some worship on Saturday evenings by going to church, others worship the bottle and head to the nearest pub. Whatever the normal ritual of your host, fall into their way of life for the few days that you are visiting and ensure their routines are not altered by your presence. Rise earlier than you normally would or amuse yourself quietly reading a magazine or going for a walk while waiting for them to wake. Check that your own showering or bathing habits will not leave the hosts without hot water.

MAKING YOURSELF SCARCE

Use travel guides and the internet to find out about places to go and things to do in the area so that you have activities to suggest. If the host indicates that you do one or more of these activities without their company, make no fuss and take part in that activity or trip without them – they may want some time to themselves.

BRING SENSIBLE CLOTHING

Even if your hosts do not mention particular garments that you may need for the weekend, give some thought as to what environment you are entering and what is sensible attire. Talk to your hosts and ask what will be needed if you are unsure. If this is not possible, make sure to take a pair of trainers, a pair of jeans, a waterproof jacket and an outfit suitable for a cocktail party.

CLEAN UP AFTER YOURSELF

The following are some useful tips if you are a guest in somebody's
home:

▶ *Don't assume that items in communal areas of the house are
there for your use, including books and CDs.*

▶ *Use a toiletries bag which can be kept in your room as
opposed to strewn around your host's bathroom.*

▶ *If you break anything, confess immediately and pay for the
damage or replace the item.*

▶ *Unless there are house staff, you must offer to help with the
washing up if your host is providing meals.*

▶ *Leave everything in the house as you have found it. Fold
towels and make the bed, even if you know the hosts
will wash everything the moment you leave.*

PAYING YOUR OWN WAY AND TREATING
YOUR HOSTS

The expense of the entire stay should not fall entirely on your
hosts, whether staying in their house or vacationing with them.
In addition to bringing a small gift on arrival and sending a
larger present when you leave, treat your hosts where possible.
Lunches or day trips are on you – they have had the inconvenience
of giving you a place to stay together with providing all
other meals.

SAYING GOODBYE

Leave before you outstay your welcome. Thank your hosts and offer to return the favour soon (even if you live in Brixton and the friends you were visiting live in the Lake District). If you must depart at an inconvenient hour, do not expect your hosts to wake in order to wave you goodbye. If they offer, insist that they stay in bed.

Special notes for the guest

SMOKING

Do not smoke in your host's house unless they light up themselves. Do not ask permission to smoke. Although your hosts may not object, do not smoke out of a window or stand smoking in a doorway as these are likely to blow smoke into the house. Go outside to smoke and shut the door behind you. Never throw your stubs in your host's garden. Request an ashtray from your host – never assume that you may use a mug or plate. Never light up before a meal is entirely finished.

Insight

If you are a smoker, set the example of where it is acceptable to smoke. Don't light up in you own house if you don't want everyone doing the same.

ALCOHOL CONSUMPTION AND APOLOGIES AFTERWARDS

Consume alcohol in moderation. If this slips your mind, try to remember that once you start slurring or falling, drink a large glass of water and go home. If a friend suggests calling you a cab, take them up on their offer. Stumbling and slurring need not be apologized for as long as you kept your good humour. If, however, when you wake you remember (or are told) that you became aggressive, sullen or that you vomited at the event, immediately apologize. Send a handwritten note and large bunch of flowers or other thoughtful gift, apologizing for hitting the bottle a little hard, perhaps saying that you were having such a good time that you lost track of what you were drinking.

DEALING WITH DRUNK GUESTS

If you notice that another guest has drunk too much alcohol, help this guest to conceal their state. Say to the drunk guest that you are getting yourself a glass of water and offer to get the drunk guest one as well. Offer your services in getting the drunk guest home by sharing a cab with them or giving them a lift.

Thank-you notes and gifts

Thank-you notes should be sent within 24 hours, but in any case, later rather than never. The form that the thank-you note should take depends on the formality of the event attended and the age of the host. If the host is under 35 and the event was casual, a text message or email will suffice. If the host is over 35 or the event was formal, a handwritten note is required. The note need not be long, but it should be personal and complimentary about the evening. For example:

> *Dear Jane and John, (omitted for text messages)*
>
> *Thank you so much for a lovely evening, your cooking really is delicious. Jim's joke about the sheep was the funniest thing I'd heard in a while.*
>
> *Hope to see you both soon,*
>
> *Jack and Jill*

For occasions where the hosts have gone to some inconvenience for you, for example because you arrived late or stayed over, the above note should be attached to a gift (see below).

GIFTS

The best gifts are those where the giver has thought about the recipient's tastes and has given something clearly well considered. There are, however, some default options that never tire: flowers, chocolates and alcohol.

Unlike gifts for special occasions, gifts given to hosts need not be wrapped and givers should not expect thank-you notes. Gifts for hosts can be given at the start of the event or delivered after the event has passed. If you want to give a gift at the event do not bring anything that will require immediate attention, such as cut flowers, but instead bring flowers pre-packaged in water or a potted plant. If you bring a present such as chocolates or wine, hand it over with a comment such as 'save them for later, you'll need them after all your hard work' or some other such nicety to explain that there is no expectation for the host to open them at that event.

10 THINGS TO REMEMBER

1 *As a guest, if accepting a dinner or lunch invitation, inform your host immediately of any special dietary requirements. As a host, do as best you can to accommodate the dietary requirements of your guests without seeming to have made a special effort.*

2 *Smoking and drug taking in your home need not be tolerated.*

3 *When having friends to stay, lay down house rules at the start.*

4 *When inviting friends on holiday, organize at the start how finances will be managed, how much time will be spent apart and what will and will not be provided.*

5 *Respond to invitations promptly.*

6 *Help hosts by trying to include shy guests in conversations or activities.*

7 *Leave or retire to bed when the host looks tired.*

8 *Pets and additional family members are not included in invitations unless specifically mentioned.*

9 *For longer stays, treat your hosts to dinners out and day trips to make up for the expense and inconvenience of having you in their home.*

10 *Always send thank-you notes or text messages afterwards.*

7

Personal appearance

In this chapter you will learn how to:
* *groom yourself*
* *dress appropriately for everyday, work, and formal occasions.*

It is often said that you should never judge a book by its cover. The trouble is, however, that a book with a colourful cover and a blurb with rave reviews in beautiful embossed writing is far more likely to capture your attention and merit a flick through than one with a grey ripped cover and a blurb so faded it is impossible to discern that it is both Richard and Judy's favourite book of the year. It is the same with people.

The unshaven guy in the supermarket with unbrushed matted hair, one purple and one grey sock, stained corduroy trousers and a torn anorak may well be a professor of astrophysics at Cambridge or equally the local tramp, but many people are unlikely to take the risk (or the time) to find out.

The professor of astrophysics may not mind being approached though and might enjoy his kookiness. In some professions, some even think that dressing down or dressing strangely is a sign of cleverness; a visual display of intellectual arrogance – a symbol that this person need not bother themselves with the trivialities of dressing appropriately as their brains negate the importance of any outward beauty. However, for most people, in addition to the case of simply making yourself more approachable, dressing well is a mark of respect to those whom you are meeting. It is also well worth noting that even the brilliant professor of astrophysics wouldn't dare turn up to lecture his students in only a thong, even if he had just discovered a ninth planet.

Below are a few rules for safe, respectful dressing and grooming. The modern lady or gentlemen may feel the need to twist an outfit for the purposes of current fashion and style, and far be it for this book to persuade otherwise. However, before pushing the limits too far, remind yourself that sometimes dressing as others would like you to is more important and respectful than dressing in a way that asserts your individuality.

Grooming

MEN AND WOMEN

Find a good hairdresser to keep your haircut up to date and visit them at the very least once every two months; once every six weeks if you can manage it. Give the hairdresser guidelines as to length but after that trust them. It may be emotionally painful for you to give up the mullet that your first girlfriend/boyfriend swooned over in the 1980s, but it's painful for everyone else to be forced to look this travesty of a haircut 20 years later. Men – be warned, even superglue won't keep your hair down on a blustery day if you choose to sport a combover.

Look after your hands and feet. Moisturize both regularly, remove rough skin and keep nails and toenails clipped, filed and clean. Don't bite the skin around your nails – bleeding fingers are as unsightly as dirty nails. Treat infections such as veruccas or warts promptly to avoid their spread to others.

Never groom in public. Not even the stronger stomached members of the public should have to keep a straight face while you pop your spots, clip your nails and ear hair and apply your foundation on the rush-hour bus. And no one but yourself should have to clean up your own stray fingernails and ear hair.

WOMEN

Remove armpit hair entirely and the hair on your legs up to wherever your shortest hemline falls. Shave, wax, epilate or burn it off with a hair removal cream while dancing to Westlife, but remove it. Equality and anti-feminism are not the issue here. Women don't want to look at your foresty legs any more than men do.

The best applied make-up is always that which looks natural. Don't be tempted to wear a darker shade of foundation than your skin colour so that you look tanned. Do remember that make-up, like haircuts, can go out of style. Throw out that frosted pink lipstick with your 1990s platform shoes.

Keep fingernails clean and of a practical length. If applying polish, consider the choice of colour carefully, choosing a light colour or French manicure for work. Darker nails can look vampish so think carefully about co-ordinating these with the rest of your outfit choice. Remove all polish as soon as it starts to chip.

Insight
> Elaborate outfits and grooming can look great, but the goal should be to look clean. Err on the side of simplicity if in doubt.

MEN

Hair removal is more about quality than quantity. If you have chosen to cultivate some form of facial topiary, keep it trimmed and tidy. If not, shave every morning and if the re-growth is fast, consider taking a travel shaving kit with you for shaving before afternoon or evening meetings. But hair removal for you is more than this. As you become older, your hair may start to migrate from your head to elsewhere on your body, leaving you bald-werewolf chic. If you are becoming more hairy, pluck your eyebrows and clip nose and ear hair.

Keep your nails short. Eddie Izzard may be able to pull off nail polish, but even in these modern times, painted fingernails on boys are not part of the well-groomed gentlemen's look. Consider visiting a manicurist in order to have hands that men want to shake and women want to hold.

> **Insight**
> Grooming is not just for girls.

Personal hygiene

MEN AND WOMEN

Shower every morning and wash your hair thoroughly, using an anti-dandruff shampoo if necessary. If you perspire a lot or have taken part in some form of exercise throughout the day, shower again. Wear a strong antiperspirant deodorant. It is not a 'glow', it is sweat, which will smell when it dries.

Wear perfume or cologne but apply with restraint so that only those hugging you can smell it. Never spray perfume or cologne in public. What you and your partner may think is sexy, others may think is anaphylactic shock-inducing and still others may think smells of cats' pee.

Wash your hands regularly throughout the day to avoid the spread of germs, but particularly after visiting the bathroom and before eating food. Use soap and lather for at least 15 seconds, paying attention to under your fingernails and the backs of your hands.

> **Insight**
> While lathering, mentally sing 'Happy Birthday' twice. That takes around 15 seconds, the amount of time you should be lathering for to truly clean your hands.

Pick your nose and ears before you leave home. If you must do this, carry it out in the confines of your own bathroom, or do it in a toilet cubicle out of sight of anyone else. Wash your hands thoroughly (as described above) afterwards.

Brush your teeth and floss. Also use mouthwash. Bad breath is often caused by the build-up of rotting food between your teeth. Consider buying a travel-sized bottle of mouthwash to use throughout the day. Take a mint whenever one is offered.

Day-to-day attire

In our choice of day-to-day clothing we reveal a tantalizing glimpse of our personalities to complete strangers. On other occasions, clothing acts as a uniform binding a group together in their formal attire.

UNDERWEAR

Underwear should be worn under clothes. Bra straps should not be seen until you are prepared to show the rest of the bra; underpants should not be visible above the trouser band; suspenders should only be worn with skirts long enough to conceal them entirely. Make sure you wear good underwear, you never know when the opportunity to show it off may arise. Greying pants are not beautiful items of clothing. Your underwear should also be functional. Measure yourself once a year for bra sizes and wear breathable underpants. Nylon gold polyester pants may look cool but they're going to make things a little fusty and moist down there.

Above all, wear underwear. Goodness know what you can spread, catch, droop or stain without it.

CASUAL CLOTHES

Casual does not mean sloppy. The best casual clothing is comfortable, weather-appropriate and looks good. It is not torn, stained or covered in holes from wear and tear.

Casual clothing can be fashionable and the options here are limitless, but regardless of whether you choose to dress as a goth or a wannabe supermodel, it must be clean, in good condition and suitable for the eyes of children. In addition, it is best not to confuse casual wear with sporting attire (see below) – tracksuits and lycra shorts are best left for sporting purposes.

Shoes should be comfortable. Depending on the occasion or task, trainers may be worn, but for events where the dress code is stated as 'casual', it is safer to wear other shoes.

Wear casual clothing for informal tasks and events such as shopping trips and visiting friends. Suitable items include anything apart from a suit jacket and tie, but it's best to avoid T-shirts with offensive wording, transparent items and skirts short enough to display cellulite.

Fabrics that are machine washable, such as denim and cotton, are the safest 'casual' attire, but more delicate items such as wool and cashmere can be worn if the design of the piece is simple (for example, no added sequins).

SPORTSWEAR

When exercising, wear clothing that is suitable for working out in and for the environment you are exercising in. Wear clothes specifically for exercising, not just your oldest most faded T-shirt. Consider wearing dark colours instead of light as they are better at concealing sweat patches. Start with a clean kit, even if you know that by the end of your exercising session you will need to wash your clothes.

Wear trainers that support your feet and underwear that supports any bits that need supporting (male or female). Stick to the house rules on the type of trainer sole allowed, as some damage the floor or court surface. Expect people to stare if you wear a skintight lycra G-string body suit ensemble, sequins or anything along a similar line. Denim is inappropriate as it is constricting.

In the gym and outdoors, items which ride up to expose more than you would like in a nightclub are not suitable.

Outdoors, wear clothing that will keep you warm enough. In the winter, wear a jogging suit, an anorak and lightweight gloves. In the summer, wear shorts and a T-shirt. Again, make sure you have the appropriate footwear.

When observing the physical pursuits of others, such as at a football game, suitable clothing is similar to that described as casual clothing above, but ramped down a notch towards outdoors sportswear and up a notch for weather suitability.

SWIMWEAR

Remember that you are on the beach or in a swimming pool, not on the set of a porn film. By all means wear bikinis and speedos (if you really must, although board shorts will win you style points) but avoid thongs and items of clothing made of leather or PVC even if it means heading to a nudist beach. Remember also that white becomes transparent when wet unless the material is heavily lined. Double check before stripping off any item of swimwear that toplessness or nudity is the accepted norm for the beach. And, if it is a nudist beach, and people all around you are baring their tan lines, when in Rome...

Never substitute lingerie for swimwear.

Insight

It is important that your swimwear fits. Any riding up or slipping down will reveal more than is decent in public.

SMART CASUAL

For men this means that you need a collar of some sort, whether it be a polo shirt or a proper shirt. Although the definition will vary according to age and occasion, it is safer to wear proper shoes (not trainers or flip flops) and a pair of full length trousers not made of denim. No tie should be worn – a jumper (not a hoody) or a cardigan will suffice, and a jacket may be worn.

For women, this means slightly more decorative dress than 'casual' attire. Simply avoid denim, trainers and hoodies.

Work attire

Depending upon the workplace, different styles of dressing will be appropriate. Fashion houses and magazines would never dream of forcing their employees' creativity into a dark suit, whereas financial services' workplaces won't let anything so casual as a polo shirt through security.

Unless there is a uniform or a dress code specified, 'safe' workplace dressing is all about the norm pre-established by those within the company. Err on the side of formality until you have become accustomed to what is acceptable attire for your place of work.

BUSINESS CASUAL

Business casual is now the standard dress code of the majority of non-financial institution offices. Teachers, doctors and journalists alike now dress in this way on a daily basis, leaving formal work attire (see below) for meetings and interviews. As a general rule:

▶ *Top half: No plunging necklines or chest hair should be visible.*
▶ *Bottom half: No jeans, combats or cargo trousers, mini-skirts (hemlines falling more than two inches above the knee) or shorts unless the dress code is specifically stated as casual.*
▶ *Shoes: No impractical high heels, flip flops or sports shoes.*
▶ *In general, avoid fluorescent colours or overly patterned or flashy items of clothing, such as those with large designer logos or sequins and shiny fabric.*

Suits are too formal for this dress code, although jackets can be worn to smarten casual outfits. Many companies define acceptable business casual attire for their employees, in which case, follow the guidelines to the letter, thinking of it as an unstructured uniform.

FORMAL BUSINESS ATTIRE

This sort of attire is worn day to day only in the least creative, most public-facing professional offices, such as those of lawyers and finance workers. Workers of other professions are also likely to wear this sort of attire to conferences or formal meetings.

Suitable articles of clothing for women include:

- ▶ *Business suits – matching bottom and top in fabric and colour; grey, black, navy; solid colour or light pinstripe; trouser suits should be tailored rather than tight; skirt or dress suits are still considered more formal but should fall one inch above the knee to mid-calf.*
- ▶ *Tights or stockings in natural colour or black, to co-ordinate with suit.*
- ▶ *Closed toe shoes – to match suit in colour, low or flat heel; no sequins or adornments.*
- ▶ *Blouse or shirt – pressed and clean; solid colours and non-distracting patterns.*
- ▶ *Wear a supportive and unnoticeable bra and minimal jewellery (stud earrings, pendant necklaces). Hair and fingernails should be clean and of natural colour and make-up unnoticeable. Avoid the display of designer labels and clothing with ruffles or styles which would be considered sexy.*

Suitable articles of clothing for men:

- ▶ *Business suit – jacket to just cover crotch and seat of trousers; grey, navy or black; solid colour or light pinstripe. Bear in mind that double-breasted suits can look sloppy when sitting.*
- ▶ *Shirt – pressed; in a dark or pastel co-ordinating colour.*
- ▶ *Vest (optional, but safer on a hot day to conceal sweat patches).*
- ▶ *Belt – black, to match shoes (avoid large flashy belts with obvious logos).*
- ▶ *Socks – dark, to co-ordinate with suit, never sports socks.*
- ▶ *Tie – pressed and co-ordinated with jacket and shirt; the tip of the tie should touch the top of the belt.*

- ▶ *Shoes – usually made of leather, black to match belt, clean and polished; no boots.*
- ▶ *Avoid designer labels on show, jewellery and flashy watches.*

JOB INTERVIEW ATTIRE

Interviewers make their decision not only on what you say (the metaphorical flick through the book) but also on your appearance and body language to ascertain whether you are suited to the job. If you are unsure as to what attire will be expected of you at interview, always err on the side of formality (i.e. formal business attire as described above). Although the dress code may be a denim delight once you start work, many interviewers may still expect you suited and booted for the judging process.

When choosing your outfit for an interview, think about what would be worn day to day for the job and theme your outfit as a smartened version of this, one notch up on the scale of formality. Wear what you would to a meeting with an important client once given the job. Many interviewers base their judgement of you on how they think their clients will perceive you. Interviewers for creative positions such as fashion designers, for example, would balk in horror at an interviewee in a grey suit and co-ordinating tie, but financial workers would immediately dismiss a candidate wearing the latest Gucci off-the-shoulder neon pink look. Whatever the position, never wear revealing clothes, trainers, sportswear or denim to a job interview.

Formal attire

WHITE TIE

White tie is the most formal evening dress code and will almost certainly be stipulated on an invitation to an event where this dress is required. Be prepared to wear white tie to dinners with visiting heads of state, hunt balls and some formal university balls.

Men should wear the following:

- ▶ *black tailcoat sharply cut away at the front and with silk facings*
- ▶ *black trousers with one or two stripes of satin*
- ▶ *white stiff-fronted shirt*
- ▶ *white stiff-wing collar*
- ▶ *white bow tie*
- ▶ *white low-cut waistcoat*
- ▶ *long black socks*
- ▶ *black patent leather shoes*
- ▶ *medals, sashes or other decorations if some military, political or royal background exists*
- ▶ *outdoors wear would comprise a black silk top hat with an opera cloak or overcoat*
- ▶ *military mess dress and formal Scottish highland dress may also be worn to white tie events.*

For women, a long formal dress and jewellery are a lady's basic white tie attire. The dress (or ball gown) is traditionally a full-skirted gown reaching at least to the ankles. If 'state decorations' are to be worn, they are on a bow pinned to the chest, and married women wear a tiara if they have one.

Although jewellery such as earrings, a necklace, rings and bracelets are advocated, a watch is not considered appropriate attire and is better kept in a clutch bag to be consulted discreetly.

Insight

White tie requires considerably more effort, and likely expense, than black tie, but the two are not interchangeable.

BLACK TIE

Black tie is worn to formal evening events. Men are expected to wear dinner jackets, otherwise known as tuxedos. Black tie is almost exclusively worn to evening functions; at some private and public dinners, dances and formal parties. Like white tie, if black tie is desired, it should be specified on the invitation. If there is any room for interpretation, a quick call to the host will save any embarrassment.

For men, the elements of a black-tie ensemble are:

- *a black short jacket with silk (ribbed) or satin lapel; single-breasted jackets have one or two buttons*
- *black trousers with one stripe of silk braid or ribbon down each leg (no belt loops or turn-ups)*
- *a white dress shirt with a pleated front (usually fastened with shirt studs and matching cufflinks)*
- *a black silk bow tie (not pre-tied, no matter how long it takes)*
- *black cummerbund (pleats facing up) or a low-cut waistcoat (optional)*
- *black socks*
- *black patent leather shoes.*

No matter the temperature, the jacket may only be removed if the highest ranking male present or host has removed theirs (if you are indeed in that happy position to make the choice, it is better to stand and remove it with a sense of showmanship in order that other men may acknowledge the implicit permission to remove their own).

Learn to tie your own bow tie. Pre-tied models are still frowned upon and, besides, nothing looks foxier than a partied-out man at 4.00 a.m. with morning stubble, his top button undone and an untied bow tie draped around the collar.

A white handkerchief (cotton, linen or silk) may be worn in the breast pocket of the dinner jacket. In cold weather a dark blue or black overcoat and a white silk scarf may be worn outdoors, but top hats are the domain of white tie only.

Military mess dress or traditional Scottish dress may be worn as an alternative to common black tie as described above.

For women, 'black tie' wear can be more diverse. Although shorter dresses may be acceptable, to err on the side of formality, an ankle or floor-length dress should be worn. Dress watches, bracelets, earrings and necklaces are all acceptable forms of accessory, and a clutch bag should be used to hold make-up and any other essentials for the evening.

Insight

As the range of outfits possible are so diverse for black tie, particularly for women, if in doubt ask the host what is acceptable, or make enquiries regarding what the hostess herself plans to wear.

COCKTAIL

Men should wear business casual with a dinner jacket. If in doubt, take business casual up a whole notch and wear a (non-pinstripe) suit and tie.

If it seems like it may be a more formal party (for example, if the invitation came by post rather than email, phone or text), it is correct to ask the host for guidance as they may be expecting black tie.

Women should wear a short (knee length or above) dress or a dressy trouser or skirt suit. Business suits do not fall under the category of cocktail attire. Embellishments such as sequins or beads are appropriate.

MORNING DRESS

Morning dress is most frequently worn by male members of a wedding party, but is also used for funerals and equestrian events such as Royal Ascot. The cutaway front of the morning coat differs from the tail coat in that the tail coat is cut horizontally across while the morning coat is cut at an oblique angle. Morning dress should only be donned during daylight hours – the equivalent formal evening wear is white tie, although modern times forgive those who do not change as the day moves into night.

Elements of morning dress include:

- *a morning coat (usually black)*
- *a waistcoat (single- or double-breasted)*
- *formal trousers (usually grey striped, no turn-up), worn with braces*
- *a double-cuffed shirt fastened with cufflinks*
- *a stiff white collar (plain turn-down or winged collar)*
- *a cravat (with winged collar) or tie (with plain turn-down collar)*
- *black dress shoes*
- *black silk or grey top hat (optional)*
- *formal gloves in suede, chamois or kid leather (optional)*
- *cane (optional)*
- *black leather (not patent leather) shoes.*

At funerals, traditionally a black or grey tie is worn, but these days that rule is less rigid.

For women accompanying a man in morning dress, a mid-calf to knee length dress or skirt should be worn. Often hats are appropriate but the use of these will be occasion-specific.

General parties

It really does depend upon the theme of the party but, whatever the dress code, make sure to embrace it whole-heartedly. This applies as much to black tie as to fancy dress. If you go to a cowboy party, no skimping on the hat or boots; for an alien party make sure your supply of green body paint is limitless; if a 'p' party, it's better to be a pirate or princess than a party pooper. If you are unsure of the dress code, ring before the party to enquire.

When unsure of what to wear

Remember the following two points:

▶ *It is never inappropriate to ask a host or other guests what may be suitable attire for an event, particularly if it is a formal one.*

▶ *If the above option is unavailable to you, it is always better to err on the side of formality. Better to arrive at a beach wedding in morning dress and have all other guests in swimwear than to arrive at a beach wedding in swimwear and have all other guests in morning dress. You can always remove a top hat, jacket and roll up sleeves and trousers; it is almost impossible to alter a casual outfit on the hop to make it look more formal.*

While it is true that there are many aspects of personality and honour that really maketh the man (or woman), dress codes allow a host to set the tone of the evening and also give guests a pre-warning as to the sort of event to expect. If an invitation states a certain dress code as optional, feel free to take the code down a notch, but not to substitute with casual or over-formal dress. For example 'black tie optional', means that a suit and tie may be worn, not jeans and a T-shirt or white tie. Similarly, informal may mean semi-formal or casual so it is worth checking with the host or other guests.

Large department stores or smaller boutiques have personal shopping assistants who are able to help in choosing outfits for formal events – dress codes are intended to provide confidence in dressing like others, so make the most of them. Learn to adhere to dress codes and never be unsuitably dressed again.

10 THINGS TO REMEMBER

1 *Groom, but not in public.*

2 *Shower every day and make sure all hair is kept clean and tidy.*

3 *Wear underwear that cannot be seen while dressed.*

4 *Casual need not mean sloppy. Dress in clean clothes and keep sportswear such as tracksuits separate from casual wear such as jeans.*

5 *If an occasion is of the sort that requires formal wear, wear it.*

6 *Don't be afraid to ask hosts the level of formality for events.*

7 *Err on the side of formality.*

8 *At work, even if the dress code is casual, keep skirts of a decent length and do not wear sportswear.*

9 *Swimwear is not underwear. Keep it decent.*

10 *Adhere to any dress codes set down by the hosts of an event.*

8

Netiquette

In this chapter you will learn how to:
- *send email*
- *blog*
- *internet date*
- *instant message*
- *take part in forum discussions.*

The rules of internet etiquette, known by boffins as 'netiquette', are evolving faster than other forms of etiquette. The years of tradition that guide these other forms of etiquette do not exist, so as technology changes and more of our lives incorporate the use of the internet, the rules governing manners in cyberspace also change.

The ultimate rule of netiquette is to adhere to similar standards of behaviour online as in person. Although it is easy to forget that other people with feelings and emotions read forum posts, emails and blogs, never say or do something on the web that you would not say or do in person.

Email

Constructing the perfect snail mail letter is childsplay, but the rules for email are still fluid. An email consists of three main parts: the recipients, the subject line and the body of the email. Each of these has its own pitfalls in the world of cyberspace etiquette.

THE RECIPIENTS

These days some people, and most professionals, spend vast amounts of time simply managing their e-inbox. At work, it's a part of the job. But both socially and at work, nobody will thank you for increasing the volume of the task by sending an email to a whole address book rather than just a few necessary contacts. Do not 'reply all' unless addressing the whole group.

BCC (blind carbon copy) recipients if, when sending to a group of people, it is important to either you or them that the recipients of the email are masked. Also BCC recipients if you want to prevent the releasing of email addresses, as they can be copied from careless e-correspondence.

The 'To' box should be used for recipients who would normally receive the letter addressed and personalized to them by snail mail. The CC function should be used for the following:

▶ *recipients whom you wish to be aware of the content of the email, without addressing the email directly to them*
▶ *recipients for whom you are happy that all receiving the email know that these recipients received the email.*

Recipients copied into the email via the CC box should not be expected to reply, although they may if they wish.

Email addresses put in the 'To' box or the 'CC' box will be accessible to all others who receive the email, so think carefully about whether they will mind this before pressing 'send'.

THE SUBJECT LINE

Keep it short and make it relevant. Think of it as a news headline. It can be funny for informal social purposes but above all, both in business and socially, use it as an opportunity to give the recipient a preview of what is in the email. Should the email be kept for reference, it will be easier to find it again if the title is relevant.

THE BODY OF THE EMAIL

This should be short and to the point, particularly at work. Emails for social purposes can be longer and, between friends, length may vary depending on the theme of the email, but if communicating a particular point, it is better to keep it short, lest the point be lost among your babble. At work, emails are always most effective if kept short (less than ten lines). Put the most important information at the start of the email in case the recipient is busy or becomes distracted. Many people read the first three lines of an email thoroughly and skim read the rest.

If you receive a long email addressed only to you, try to read the whole thing, not just the first three lines.

Do not write in capital letters. People will think you are shouting, angry, or worse still, that you are too stupid to realize that you have turned on the Caps Lock. Write with all the civilities you would normally attach to a short formal letter, but without the addresses at the top of the page. If the letter is for business purposes, keep your form of address and sign-off formal, as you would in snail mail. For social purposes, it's up to you to determine how you want to address your friends, but it is wise not to use text speak on any email, professional or social, as it often makes the message more difficult to read.

Although emailing, like letter writing, is often used to say that which you are too scared to say in person, never write anything in an email that you feel would be too harsh for you to say in person.

Email attachments

Attach large files to emails only when you are sure that the recipient will be pleased to receive the file, as they can take a long time to download. Label attachments with a clear description of their contents to avoid unwanted downloads.

When sending several photos as attachments, consider setting up a website for the photos (there are many free photo-sharing websites available on the internet that are easy to use) and emailing the link rather than the actual photos.

Extra email functions

Only use email functions to denote a message as urgent (i.e. attach the red flag or exclamation mark) if it truly is time-sensitive.

Do not request read receipts for every email. Use only for emails which are time-sensitive or for important information sent to people who check their email irregularly.

Do set up an out-of-office auto-reply to your business email if you are away from email checking facilities for longer than half a day. The auto-reply should give the expected time and date of your return and a contact number or email address of a colleague who may be able to help in the meantime.

Miscellaneous email etiquette

If you have requested something via email, it is nice to send a 'thank you' to acknowledge its receipt. It is, however, not necessary to thank a thank you, or even to reply 'you're welcome'.

Like any correspondence, reply to emails as soon as possible. If an email requests a reply by return, click the reply button and write something, no matter how short, to acknowledge receipt and answer what you can. If the email does not request a reply by return, use personal judgment to decide in which order to reply to emails, although it is sensible to order your replies by their level of urgency. Endeavour to reply to all business emails within half a day of receipt and social emails within the day or at the very least, send a short apology to explain the delay. Always spell check before you send.

When forwarding or replying to messages, always edit. Don't send a message with your signature or anyone else's repeated, or send messages attached to your own that the recipient has no need to read. If an email has been erroneously addressed to you and is clearly not spam, reply to explain that the mail should be redirected. Do not reply to spam.

Remember that although email sending and receiving is almost instant, the speed of reply will depend mostly upon how often a person checks their email account. These days, professionals should check their email at least once every hour; non-professionals a minimum of twice a day.

Never forward or create email messages threatening any sort of misfortune should the recipient not continue the forwarding to a designated number of people. If you are daft enough to fall for it yourself, at least delete the bit that threatens death and destruction before you press send.

As email manners are ever-changing, it is unlikely that a person will think you despicably rude should you not adhere strictly to the above. However, use the above to present yourself as smarter than the average email basher.

Insight

Although email has its advantages in speed, it cannot replace the personal touch of a handwritten letter. When writing to those where the sentiment of the letter is more important than that timing of the receipt, send a handwritten letter via snail mail.

Blogging

A blog (a portmanteau of web log) … provides commentary or news on a particular subject such as food, politics or local news; some function as more personal online diaries.

Wikipedia definition of 'blog', 1 September 2007

Blogging is no longer the territory of the technological cutting edge. With the domination of Facebook and MySpace, it is now the territory of the uprising star, the wannabe newspaper columnist and the near-on raving lunatic.

The trouble with blogging is this: you may blog about anything you please. You can write about politics, new technology, festivals, your pets, your cat's incontinence, your belief that the world is indeed controlled by a six-legged octopus in the sky. Anything. And herein lies the problem.

Blogging is public speaking for techhie/writer hybrids. If you wouldn't say it in public, don't say it on your blog. Your cat might not be offended should she read over your shoulder that you have broadcast her penchant for humping the next-door neighbour's feline friend. Your grandmother, on the other hand, may be horrified to hear that you have told an avid internet audience of her frolicking with the next door neighbour. Think before you write. Blogs are a public diary, not a private diary. Pause, ponder the ramifications, keep it clean and re-read for typing errors. Then post.

Facebook

Facebook is a 'social networking site', combining blogging with direct communication via an ability to link to the facebooks of friends. Facebook has recently found favour across the globe and across the generations. Other such sites, for example Bebo and MySpace have enjoyed some fame but for the moment at least, Facebook seems the site set to shift the standard method of social internet communication away from email. Whether it is a flash in the pan idea or here to stay remains to be seen, but such is its widespread popularity that no guide to internet etiquette can now be complete without its mention.

As Facebook becomes more commonly used as a form of communication rather than a tool for photo sharing, the rules of etiquette are rapidly firming. The main components are:

- ▶ *photos: the profile photo and tagged photos*
- ▶ *personal information*
- ▶ *the wall (messages public to all)*
- ▶ *the homepage (providing information about the goings on of your friends' walls and changes in personal information, seen only by you)*
- ▶ *the inbox (messages seen only by you)*
- ▶ *groups*
- ▶ *event invitations*
- ▶ *the friend list.*

THE PROFILE PHOTO AND TAGGED PHOTOS

Use a clear, recent, non-offensive (choose one that you wouldn't mind your grandmother seeing) picture on your profile page. Attention John Smith – it is going to be difficult to find you without it.

You may 'tag' photos of your friends so that they appear on the photo page of your tagged friends' Facebook profiles. Do not tag pictures of friends engaged in scandalous, adulterous or criminal activity. Remember that partners and potential employers also have access to the internet. Tagging a picture of a friend vomiting while grasping a bottle of Ouzo with one hand and a topless model with the other may not seem so funny when you find out your friend's wife has moved out and they have been declined their dream job as a vodka sales rep.

Insight

If unsure about which photos your friends will want tagged, upload the album and send a message to friends in the album telling them to tag themselves.

Do not upload photos of your friends that will clearly land them in trouble even if you refrain from tagging them. Depending on how your privacy settings are managed on your Facebook account, unexpected viewers may still see these by flicking through the whole online album.

PERSONAL INFORMATION

Feel free to put what you like here as long as it is not offensive to anyone else, for example in the form of racism. Be decisive and limit your list of favourite music, hobbies, etc. to no more than ten items each.

The 'relationship status' information can be the cause of many Facebook troubles. When setting up your Facebook account, if you choose to set the relationship status to 'single', the establishment of a relationship does require the change of this status as a mark of respect to your new partner, no matter how showy this may seem. The new status need not elaborate on the details of the newly fledged romance, and may in fact simply change to a neutral position. However, it will need to be changed so that is does not blare singledom to all and sundry.

Likewise, if the relationship status reads 'In a relationship with Jane Smith', no matter the pain of seeing the broken heart icon pop onto your screen and the homepages of everyone else, upon the demise of a relationship, you will need to change the status. It is courteous for the dumper to let the dumpee change their relationship status first. If either of the above seems too sick-making or heart-breaking, simply do not set the relationship status in the first place.

The 'looking for' tab may be set to whatever you please. Partners may not grumble should you choose to set it to read 'looking for whatever I can get'.

THE WALL (PUBLIC TO ALL) AND THE INBOX (MESSAGES SEEN ONLY BY YOU)

Remember that the Facebook wall is a publicly accessible entity. Other people can see it. Do not post notes on a friend's wall which give away secrets; send a private message to their inbox instead. It is not nice to use Facebook wall messages to make a partner jealous.

Reply to messages and wall posts in a timely manner. As Facebook surfing is a leisure activity, the acceptable reply time for a Facebook message is longer that that of emails. Use one week as a guideline, although be aware that students/the unemployed/known Facebook addicts may expect a quicker response. If you require an urgent response, send an email or call.

GROUPS

Before adding another group, check to see whether one with the same purpose already exists. If so, instead of creating a new group, join that one instead.

EVENT INVITATIONS

Invitations to events have a built-in RSVP function. Use it. There's the option of 'yes', 'no' or 'maybe'. Give your response some thought and don't check 'maybe' every time. Everyone knows you are waiting for a better offer. It won't make you popular. Often, people are trying to gauge numbers of attendees so reply before the event. Although it is often tempting to only write excuses for non-attendance on the wall of the event, if time is abundant, also post positive messages such as 'really looking forward to it', so that the organizer does not merely have a stream of negative replies.

THE FRIEND LIST

It is perfectly acceptable to decline the friendship requests of work colleagues should you wish to keep work and play apart. However, if you want to do so, you must decline everyone at work, giving a short explanation. Likewise, if someone rejects you, take the hint.

'Number of friends' is not indicative of how popular you are in the real world. Don't invite everyone you've ever spoken to – request the 'friendship' of only those whose lives you genuinely are interested in. Accept 'friendship' from everyone apart from those whom you genuinely dislike or do not know.

- ▶ *Don't check your Facebook account at work, unless during a lunch break.*
- ▶ *It is okay to poke people on Facebook. It is not friendly in real life.*
- ▶ *Facebook stalking, although possible, is a terrifying potential reality. Nobody likes thinking that their footsteps around the world can be traced with alarming accuracy. If you want to see someone and you have resorted to these tactics, do yourself and them a favour and don't admit to it.*
- ▶ *Don't dump your partner or give any other bad news on Facebook, particularly not on their wall. Facebook is a place where friends get together and keep in touch in cyberspace. It should not be a place of sadness.*

Instant messaging

Faster than an email and less disruptive than taking a phone call, instant messaging can be a timesaver if used appropriately. The trouble with IM though, is that it often does not live up to its marketing. It is very often disruptive, time consuming and, shock, horror, not instantaneous.

If a person is busy, they will probably not answer the phone and ignore their email, choosing instead to return a call or email later. No one is offended – the assumption is that the person is away from their desk or, as is the case, too busy to be interrupted. In the real world, people don't tend to disrupt those who show signs of being otherwise occupied – typing frantically or talking to another group of people for example. The trouble with instant messaging stems from its oblivious intrusiveness. Screens flash, a booo-booop sound is made and the instant messenger programme does all it can to get your attention in the manner of an unruly child, with no thought to whether the recipient is on a deadline or a coffee break.

A few guidelines for IM usage can, however, grasp it back from the clutches of boredom and irritation. Try the following:

▶ *Say 'hello' and 'goodbye'. It's rude not to in real life and the same goes for the virtual world. Always start a conversation by asking if the other person is busy and giving an explanation of the purpose of the chat. This will give the other person a chance to evaluate the importance of the chat with respect to what they are occupied with. Saying goodbye signals the end of the conversation. Not saying goodbye on IM is like tiptoeing away from a conversation when the other person's back is turned.*

▶ *If you IM in a place with others around, for example a work office, turn off the beeping noise. You don't need it to alert you (and inadvertently everyone else) to the message – the flashing icon will suffice.*

▶ *Type quickly and in short bursts. It is better to send the first half of a sentence and complete it in a second message, than force your correspondent to wait for a long chunk which will take a large amount of digestion.*

▶ *Don't write in capitals unless you intend to shout.*

▶ *Don't IM with more people than you can maintain a sensible stream of conversation with. For most, the limit is two before the responses become delayed and confused.*

▶ *Do use IM rather than email to send files to avoid crowding inboxes.*

▶ *Typing is tiring – if the conversation looks like it may be a long one, suggest a phone call instead.*

▶ *Keep an eye on questions which may have been written as you write and respond as soon as you can to show that you have noticed.*

▶ *Only use nicknames for personal IMing purposes. At work, or at home if you are using your actual name (especially if it is a common one such as 'Dave'), add your surname. It will make contact easier as no matter how distinctive you are in person, perhaps with ten nose rings, a tattoo of the queen and a lovely sense of humour, people do struggle to differentiate between the first, second and fourteenth Dave on their list of contacts.*

▶ *Check the other person's presence status. Don't start the onslaught of flashing and beeping if the other person is clearly stated as 'busy'. Equally, update your own status to reflect your availability, adding a comment if necessary to clarify your situation. Some people consider the 'busy' status as a 'do not interrupt'; others as an 'only interrupt if important'. If the request is urgent and important, consider IMing, but do not expect a prompt response.*

▶ *Do not overuse abbreviations. It doesn't make you look cool, it makes you look like a poor writer. Abbreviations should be used to increase efficiency, not to decrease it. Consider whether the person you are IMing with is likely to understand the abbreviation you are using and if not, don't use it.*

Insight

There is often no replacement for hearing someone's voice. Although IMing may be more convenient, do make the effort to call occasionally or make a visit, particularly when the subject matter being discussed is confusing or is likely to elicit some emotional response.

Twitiquette

The concept of Twitter is simple. Say what you are doing in 140 characters or less. As a simple messaging platform, even simpler than a blog, the etiquette should be simple. But as with many forms of internet communication there is great potential for misuse and causing offence, perhaps even more so with Twitter because the platform is specifically designed for those on the move when a multitude of distractions can make slipping up easy. Here are a few pointers to help your tweets sing:

▶ *Stick to the 140 character word limit, but see it as a challenge to be concise rather than an opportunity to create your own abbreviations. Use only abbreviations that are commonly known, such as 'u' for 'you' and always use numerals rather than words. If you commonly need a longer message, consider starting a blog instead. Do try to watch spelling, punctuation and grammar – using correct capitalization will not waste precious characters. As you are answering the question 'What are you doing?' there is no need to start your response with 'I am'.*

▶ *Unless you work for a news service, don't provide a running commentary of events such as football games. Restrict your posting to commenting on notable points of the event or hourly updates. For example, post when someone scores a goal, not when every pass is made or even every attempt at a goal is tried.*

▶ *Give careful thought as to whether to use an @reply or a direct message. Use @replies only when adding to a public conversation. When saying something only one or two people will understand or care about, or giving a simple reply such as 'yes' or 'no', use direct messaging. Give all messages more thought than replying to a direct message with a direct message or an @reply with an @reply.*

▶ *Don't steal someone else's tweet and claim it as your own. When re-tweeting, to give credit to the idea, add RT@ originalusername as a prefix to the message.*

▶ *Think about where you are when twittering. Don't twitter in places where you wouldn't use your mobile phone on silent, for example funerals.*

▶ *It is no longer necessary to follow all users that follow you (this was different at the start when there was a much smaller group of people using Twitter). Reciprocating following is voluntary but remember that close friends will probably be a bit miffed if you make it clear that you don't think there is much they have to say of interest.*

▶ *Excessive plugging of yourself or your work counts as spamming in Twitter-land. If you must do this on Twitter, dilute the plugs with real messages, but restrain yourself in your tweeting in general. There is such a thing as too much of a good thing – go for quality not quantity.*

▶ *The only exception to the plugging rule is if you have set up a Twitter account in the name of a business or product, in which case plug away.*

- ▶ *Do not forget that Twitter is public and can be read by anyone, so don't complain about your work, your boss, your friends or your flatmate unless you are happy for them to read about it. Remember to be vague about parties where only a few people are invited and be careful when involving the opinions of others. Be particularly careful if tweeting drunk.*
- ▶ *Stop following people whenever you want to. There is no need to send a break-up tweet.*
- ▶ *Remember that Twitter is not Facebook. Synchronizing your Twitter and Facebook accounts so that they have the same status updates is wrong. Have an original thought for each or don't bother to update one of them.*

Internet dating

Internet dating is dating and most of the same rules apply once you have got to the point of a second meeting. However, there are some points of etiquette that apply specifically to internet dating highlighted here. Some are a matter of safety and others just pure courtesy.

Insight

It is unfair to use unsuspecting internet dates as an escort service. If this is your intention, make it clear before meeting up.

BEFORE A DATE

Everyone likes to present themselves in a favourable light, but don't lie. By all means use a nice picture of yourself, but touching up with Photoshop is cheating, as is using a photo that is 20 years old or one of someone else entirely.

Don't try to make yourself more attractive by listing activities that you are not genuinely interested in. Likewise, don't fake interest in the activities of others. Like real dating, give the most real depiction of yourself possible while highlighting what you think are your most likeable aspects.

If you like the look of someone, check their profile to see if you fit the description of the sort of person they are looking for. If you don't match, get over it. Move on. Don't send a message on the off chance. One day, you really will find someone who wants a 43-year-old oboe-playing Buddhist smoker, but it probably won't be that hot deaf Jewish lung cancer specialist who's looking for someone between 25 and 30 years old with a similar view on life.

Both men and women may request dates. There is no need to be coy. Clearly you are internet dating to look for romance. Upon the first request for an internet date, it is not necessary to reply if the answer is 'no'. That much is assumed. Don't repeatedly try to contact the same person if you do not receive a response.

Be safe and respect the safety of others. Don't put information on an internet dating site which could lead strangers to finding out your place of work or where you live. Use an assumed surname if necessary. If you do manage to find other contact details for someone other than those provided on the internet dating site, do not use them – many people like to keep their internet dating lives separate from their day-to-day existence until a real relationship emerges.

DATING

Have several phone conversations and/or instant messaging dates before agreeing to meet someone in person. When an arrangement to meet is made, meet somewhere public, preferably in daylight. Stay for at least an hour and don't leave without saying goodbye. Always tell a friend where you are going and a time to call to check that all is well. Do the same for your second and third dates. Conceal your exact address for as long as it takes for the other person to gain your trust.

If you have set a face-to-face date with someone, treat them with the same respect as you would a normal first date. Turn up on time and make an effort with what you are wearing. If the need to cancel arises, give the other person as much warning as possible.

WHEN IT DOESN'T WORK OUT

After a few dates, if neither of you shows signs of wanting to continue the romance, it is acceptable to simply stop emailing. If one party shows signs of wanting to continue, a rejection note will be necessary. If you are the one doing the rejecting, there is no need for an analysis of the other person's faults. 'I don't think we are suited' is far better than 'On reflection I think that you talk too much, particularly about your mother; I'm sure I can smell a sweating cow when you wear your favourite leather trousers; and you have a large nose.'

Don't try to turn an internet dating relationship into just a friendship without letting the other person know. As you met under the potential of romance, this is leading the other person on.

Forum etiquette

Forums are places of debate and wisdom. Acting as a virtual family, forum members can ask questions and have problems solved and advice given on any topic from childbirth to open-source software creation. As intellectually nurturing a place as a forum can be, it is easy to forget that by participating in a forum, you are taking part in a group discussion with real people and as such, breaches of forum etiquette happen frequently. Bear the following in mind when using forums, no matter how familiar you become with them.

- ▶ *Control your emotions – don't attack in public. If someone has in some way offended you on an internet forum, keep your temper, apply to the administrator of the forum to have the post removed and make contact with the offender via email to sort the problem out privately.*
- ▶ *Stay on topic – pay attention to the topic of the thread and the forum on which you are posting. If you do not think that your message relates, find somewhere else to post your thoughts. It is rude to make others wade through a series of off-topic posts to find the part they actually want to read. If you cannot find an appropriate thread, start a new one titling it in a way that makes its content clear.*
- ▶ *Hold your temper with newcomers – although they might be frustrating. Not knowing forum etiquette, they ask questions to which the answers are obvious or easy to find, they post in the wrong places and don't make their answers clear. Be patient and nudge (rather than push) them in the right direction by kindly pointing out their mistakes. They'll get better with a little guidance and may eventually become valuable forum members.*
- ▶ *Abbreviations – only use abbreviations that all who read the forum will understand. Use them to improve the speed of reading and writing of the forum, not to hinder it.*
- ▶ *Don't beat a dead horse – do not reopen controversial decisions you disagree with unless you have significant new information which will likely change the final decision on the matter. Without any new information, the same rounds of debate will simply be repeated and likely reach the same conclusion.*
- ▶ *Don't crosspost – find the most specific thread or forum for your question. Don't post a message on a general forum if you can find a more specific outlet for your thoughts.*
- ▶ *No large attachments – do not post large attachments as they make the web pages slow to load, particularly for people with slow network connections. If you have a large file that you would like to distribute, put it on a separate web page and post the link to the web page instead.*
- ▶ *Quoting material – do not quote the whole message to which you are replying. Re-post only enough to provide context.*

Some people/forums tend to quote first and then reply; others reply and then include the quote to which they are responding below; others still break up the quoted material with their response. There is nothing innately wrong with any of these methods, but it is polite to observe and comply with the convention of the forum you are using.

▶ *Simple is best – respond clearly and concisely in a plain-text format, if possible, which will be legible to the maximum number of people.*

THE RULES OF INDIVIDUAL FORUMS

Most forums have their own rules. Read them before you start posting and adhere to them once you do start to post. In particular, note the rules for unsubscribing and test messages to avoid irritating other forum users.

Miscellaneous rules of internet etiquette

Never:

▶ *Send viruses knowingly. Keep your virus checker up to date to avoid the spread of viruses unknowingly.*
▶ *Assume a false identity to cyber stalk an ex-lover, colleague or friend.*
▶ *Hack an email account other than your own without permission – this behaviour is as unacceptable as someone intercepting your snail mail.*

Insight
Be patient with others. The internet has its own code of conduct which is difficult for newcomers to understand. If others do something to offend, confuse, or make things difficult, do send a private message to let them know what the right thing is to do.

10 THINGS TO REMEMBER

1   *Consider carefully who to put in the To box, the Cc box and the Bcc box.*

2   *Write the subject line as a news headline. It can be funny, but let it have some link to the message in the body of the email.*

3   *Blogs serve as public diaries. Consider the ramifications of what is written in these being in the public domain.*

4   *Never tag photos or write messages in a public forum which could seriously embarrass the subject of the photos or damage their career.*

5   *Don't write personal messages in public internet spaces.*

6   *Use phones for long conversations, not IM.*

7   *In public areas, turn off the bleeping noise of IM.*

8   *Never hack into another person's email account.*

9   *Never send viruses knowingly.*

10 *Stay on topic in forums.*

9

Travelling

In this chapter you will learn how to:
- *travel by car, air and sea*
- *be a foreigner.*

By land, sea or air, travelling has a tendency to become a stressful business as hordes of people check in, scramble for seats and lose their tempers. Now air travel has become cheaper, journeying to far-off lands has become a regular activity, with some people even commuting between countries on a daily basis. However, whether setting off on a trip to the Amazon or simply navigating the delights of the M25, the tips below should help you to add courtesy to the commotion.

Travel by car

ETIQUETTE FOR DRIVERS

The rules of good behaviour as a driver are great in number, but luckily they can all be found in 'The Highway Code', knowledge of which should be refreshed periodically. Follow this rulebook to the letter and you'll never be considered a rude driver. In particular, note the use of horns (only as a warning and never as a vent for road rage) and disposal of litter (never out of the window of a moving vehicle even if it is biodegradable).

ETIQUETTE FOR ALL IN THE CAR

Basic rules:

- ▶ *When travelling with others, agree on how to share expenses for the trip (petrol money, etc.) before you start, as well as duties such as map reading and how many hours each of you can drive for without becoming drowsy.*
- ▶ *As a passenger, keep backseat driving to a minimum – if you believe the driver is endangering the health of all in the car, insist they be more cautious, but leave all decisions on routes to the driver or map reader if one has been designated.*
- ▶ *As a passenger, don't sleep in a car unless the driver makes it clear that he or she will be fine without company.*
- ▶ *During the trip, choices in music should accommodate the tastes of everyone in the car, not just the person in the driving seat.*
- ▶ *Neither drivers nor passengers should consume alcohol. Passengers under the influence can be distracting and thus as dangerous as a drunk driver.*
- ▶ *Everyone should wear a seatbelt for the safety of all in the car. The driver has every right to refuse to set off until everyone has buckled up.*
- ▶ *Keep your temper. Even if a wrong turn was taken and an hour of travelling time has been added, you'll get there in the end, and with considerably better spirits if you just let it go.*
- ▶ *If your temper frays to breaking point because of another driver's sloppy car handling, remember that most bad drivers are stupid rather than mean-spirited and expressing your road rage will brand you uncontrolled and impatient.*

Insight

Travelling is especially tiring for the driver. If a driver says that he or she is tired, always encourage a rest rather than ploughing on in order to reach a destination sooner.

Travel by air

BEFORE TRAVELLING

Most airlines have strict guidelines as to what and how much you are allowed to take on board and pack in your hold luggage. This information will be on your tickets and on the airline's website. Adhere to the guidelines. Weigh and measure your bags if you are unsure as to whether you are breaching weight or size restrictions. Put your passport and tickets in an easily accessible pocket in your hand luggage, so as to not hold up the long, winding check-in queue.

No matter how early your flight is, have a shower the morning you travel and apply deodorant. Sitting next to someone with stale body odour in a confined space is a particularly unpleasant experience.

AT THE AIRPORT

If for some reason, you make it to the front of the check-in queue with bags of size and/or weight unacceptable to the airline, don't argue. The plea that your bathroom scales read differently or that you thought the rules for size measurements were in inches, not centimetres, will fail and you will delay all the irritable people (who may have packed their cases properly) behind you. Grit your teeth and accept the fine and directions to the oversize baggage check-in without a tantrum.

At the check-in desk, have your passport and tickets ready for inspection. Although it may not be possible to accommodate your request, you may express a preference for an aisle or window seat. However, if you request a particular seat number, expect it to be regarded with raised eyebrows unless you offer some qualifying statement (such as, 'I had that seat on my last trip and the view of the television was perfect'). You may also request a seat by an emergency exit which usually has more leg room, but no matter how long your legs, don't expect that your request will always be accommodated – you have no prior claim and those seats are in high demand, usually given to parents with small children. Also, be prepared that some airlines charge more for these seats. If you are gutsy and well dressed enough to ask whether a free upgrade is available, be prepared to smile and laugh when the assistant says no.

At the security point before you enter the departure lounge, there are usually signs to indicate what will need to pass through the X-ray scanner and what may remain on your person. To avoid delaying others, before you reach the scanner, remove the items to be scanned (normally your hand luggage will need to be zapped, together with the contents of your pockets, belts, laptops, coats and any liquids, but the regulations do change), and walk through the body scanner.

If any of your hand luggage is deemed to contain items unsuitable for travelling onboard, those items will be confiscated. Don't fight for your half bottle of whiskey, silver engraved scissors or Dior perfume – the security guards have heard it all before and you will not achieve anything apart from making a scene.

However much time you think is reasonable to allow for checking in, double it. As a result of thorough security checks and a tedious but necessary checking-in procedure, getting through the airport and onto the plane has a nasty habit of always taking longer than you think, causing stress and intolerance of others. If you leave excessive time to get to the airport and through it, miraculously you won't be tempted to jump the check-in or departure-lounge queue. That old lady in front of you rummaging around in her extra large bag won't even seem to sprout devil's horns as she finds her spare false teeth, incontinence pads, medications, spare underwear, toothbrush, toothpaste, diary, book, alarm clock, kitchen sink and plumber but not her passport. You will be the picture of good manners and etiquette without breaking a sweat about catching your plane.

If you are indeed blessed and manage to pass through the queues and checks at lightning speed, the departure lounge will always provide some entertainment.

While waiting to board at the gate, do not put your carry-on luggage on the chairs if they are limited and passengers are standing. Keep mobile phone conversations to a minimum at the gate. Switch off your phone before you board the plane and do not turn it on again until you are inside the terminal building at your destination. At the gate, wait for your seat to be called before you try to board the plane – trying to sneak onto the flight early will result in a people traffic jam.

ABOARD THE PLANE

Basic rules:

▶ *When boarding the plane, weaving your way down the aisles, carry your luggage in front of you rather than over your shoulder to avoid bashing those already seated. If you are seated adjacent to an aisle, keep your elbows and feet well inside your seating space.*

▶ *If the seats are unallocated, be considerate when seating yourself. For example, don't sit in the middle of a row of three seats, potentially splitting up the seating of two people travelling together.*

▶ *Once aboard, be considerate of those trapped on the plane with you – in particular the person in front, behind and next to you:*

▷ *Do not take off your shoes, subjecting your fellow passengers to the stench of your sweaty shoes and socks. Wear shoes to travel in that will easily accommodate the expansion of your feet with the altitude.*

▷ *Before you recline your seat for the first time, lean over and ask the person behind you whether they mind. If they do grant you permission (and they likely will, having been shocked by such a display of unexpected manners), only recline the seat for as long as you need to sleep, returning it to its vertical position at all other times during the flight, and particularly if the person behind you is using his or her pull-down tray to eat or work.*

▷ *Don't kick the seat in front of you or use the headrest to pull yourself up – both of these will disturb the person in the seat in front with a violent jerking motion.*

▷ *Some people like to chatter on planes and make new friends. Others aren't so keen. When you arrive at your seat on the plane, outstretch your hand and introduce yourself, adding an additional comment about the weather or how crowded the plane is. Then sit down. If the other person would like to talk, they'll probably say something animatedly. If they don't, they won't respond with vigour, preferring to give a shorter answer. If you find yourself in the unhappy position of being seated next to a chatterbox when you would prefer to sleep or stare into the distance, note that short responses to questions, a lack of enquiry on your side and a swift application of earphones (even if there is no music playing) should send the right message of 'do not disturb'.*

▷ *Don't stand in the aisles to have long conversations with friends. When standing, keep your chatter brief. Although talk between two people sitting together is almost inaudible, conversation between someone standing and someone sitting is disturbing, and you may be blocking the view of the television for some passengers.*

▷ *Each person on the plane should have one armrest. If you seem to have two, you are using too many at the irritation of someone else.*

▷ *Keep strict control of your alcohol consumption. Drunk people on planes are a nuisance to both flight attendants and passengers.*

▷ *When using the toilet, take care to leave it the way you found it.*

▷ *If you are using a personal music or DVD player, check with the person next to you that noise from your headphones is not audible. If you are using a laptop, ask whether the clicking noise from the keys is disturbing. If the person next to you has a laptop on, do not ask them what they are working on in an effort to make polite conversation. Chances are, if they are doing it in the* cramped conditions of a plane, it's urgent for when they land and they will be working against the clock (or rather the laptop's limited battery life).

▷ Think twice before pressing the button requesting attention from a flight attendant. They are very busy and are looking after a vast number of people each. If possible, leave your request until one of the attendants walks past.

▷ If you have children, most passengers will understand that they will be difficult to keep quiet on a long-haul flight but, as parents, you have a duty to the other passengers to control their havoc wreaking. Bring games, books and non-noisy toys to keep them entertained and don't let them run in the aisles, play with their chair's recline function or kick the back of the chair in front.

▷ If you are a couple, leave passionate kissing to spaces less confined than these, and abandon plans for even chaste kissing if there is anyone in the seat next to either of you. Do not indulge in anything further under the cover of a blanket – you will be spotted. If the desire to join the mile high club is all-consuming, find your way to the toilet (men first), and try it there. If you are rumbled and there is a knocking on the door, you must finish whatever you're up to immediately and sheepishly remove yourselves from the toilet cubicle as quickly as possible.

Insight
Be speedy in the aeroplane's bathroom, even if you are on your own. If there is a queue, leave retouching your make-up and brushing your teeth until there is no queue or to be done in the airport's facilities after you land.

AT YOUR DESTINATION

When you land, don't queue jump or push in order to leave the plane quickly. Allow enough space at the luggage conveyor belt for everyone to identify and take their bags. Help those who are nearby with large bags, particularly women, the elderly and those with children.

Travel by train and bus

Like all forms of travel, allowing extra time to get to the station, buy your ticket and catch your train or bus will undoubtedly make you a friendlier, better-mannered person.

Basic rules:

▶ *At the station, buy a ticket or collect a ticket before you travel. The people who check your ticket on the train or bus should be a last resort for purchase, not an assumed method.*

▶ *On the train or bus, stow baggage in the luggage racks or baggage compartments available. Leaving large bags near you will obstruct the aisles and thus the passage of ticket collectors and other passengers.*

▶ *If you have a handbag or rucksack with you, do not put it on the seat next to you unless there is an abundance of free seats available – your bag does not have the same rights as a ticket-holding passenger and does not deserve a seat if there are people standing. Put it on the floor before you need to be asked. On public transport it is fair to ask a person to move their bags from a seat that you wish to sit in if availability is limited.*

▶ *Don't eat hot or smelly foods and do clean up after yourself, removing all wrappers and empty containers.*

▶ *Smoking on trains and buses is not permitted.*

▶ *Sit with your legs together to avoid exposing a body area most of the public have no desire to see and encroaching on a fellow passenger's personal space.*

▶ *Put your mobile phone on silent. If you need to use it, speak quietly and keep the conversation short.*

▶ *Train or bus toilets tend to be pretty grim, but don't leave them in a worse state than you found them.*

▶ *If you are travelling with children, keep them under control. Bring toys to keep them entertained and don't let them run around screaming and wreaking havoc.*

- *Keep the volume on your personal music player low. When setting the volume, take your earphones out and hold them an arm's length away. If you can still hear noise, it is too loud.*
- *If you are sharing a table with someone, only use your half. Do not succumb to the temptation of sprawling out newspapers, magazines, food and books simply because you were the first to arrive.*
- *Do not put your feet on the seats. The fabric may look as though it is in a significantly less hygienic state than the soles of your shoes, but the practice of putting your feet on seats is still frowned upon.*

Follow aeroplane etiquette for guidelines on talking to other passengers on long journeys (see page 119).

> **Insight**
> Be alert. Offer your seat to those who need it more than you do and do offer to move to another seat if it means that travelling companions can sit together.

Travel by sea

CRUISE SHIPS

On a cruise you live on a floating island with many of the same amenities and activities that you find in your hometown. Although you are on holiday, practise the same rules of etiquette as you would at home in shops, gyms, shows and other public places.

Dress code is as important for fitting in on a cruise ship as it is for everyday wear on-shore. Follow the guidelines for attire set out by the cruise ship's itinerary, or ask the cruiseline about dress codes for activities and events. Pack sensibly for a range of weather conditions as well as swimwear and items for a few more formal evening events – pack what you would for the same length of time at a top hotel at a beach resort during monsoon season. Unless the itinerary specifies a formal event, evening wear will likely be more along the style of business casual than black tie. Think carefully about packing minimally, particularly if you are sharing a cabin with someone, as space is often limited. At all times be clean and hygienic and err on the side of formality.

Basic rules:

▶ *Don't queue jump to board the ship.*
▶ *Once aboard ship, if you need to traverse the hallway at night or during the day, dress appropriately, not in nightwear or underwear.*
▶ *Do not put personal items on a chair or sun lounger in order to reserve it for your use later on in the day. You may leave your personal items on a lounger without accompanying them yourself for 15 minutes at an absolute maximum. Any longer is selfishly hogging.*
▶ *Mind your children. They may not seem as adorable to everyone else as they do to you, and leaving them to cause havoc on a ship by running around freely and splashing in the pool is inconsiderate of other passengers as well as unsafe. When they seem overexcited, find a calming activity or take them back to the cabin until they are less hyperactive.*
▶ *If there are smoking areas, make sure you smoke within them.*
▶ *Be aware of rules about running and jogging on the ship's deck with regard to safety as well as time of day. The rules may exist to avoid disturbing those on the floor below. If you participate in a cruise ship group exercise or other activity, make an effort to be there on time.*
▶ *Mind your noise levels. Wear headphones to listen to music in public places on the ship rather than using portable speakers. In your cabin, keep the volume low on music and televisions as the walls are thin. Close doors carefully – don't slam them, particularly late at night or early in the morning.*
▶ *Avoid excessive drinking. Terrible hangovers are likely to make you ill-mannered and coupled with the motion*

of the ocean, your nausea is likely to make the journey uncomfortable for more people than just yourself.

▶ *Listen when a crew member gives instructions to avoid having to ask questions later.*

▶ *Leave complaints about problems which staff clearly cannot fix to when you are home and can put them in writing, for example if the ship needs to take an unexpected detour or experiences a mechanical failure. At the time, if there are minor problems which the crew can help with (and try to remember that they cannot fix the weather), ask them nicely for their assistance. Try to maintain your good humour to avoid forcing others into listening to your whining.*

▶ *If you disembark at any point, ensure that you know what time you are expected back on the ship to avoid worry or the ship departing without you.*

▶ *Tip as you would in day-to-day life.*

▶ *If the ship lays out any additional rules, obey them.*

YACHTS

Basic rules:

▶ *Bring soft luggage rather than hard cases, as soft luggage is easier to store. Pack lightly as storage space will be limited.*

▶ *The captain sets the ground rules. As he or she is responsible for all aspects of safety on-board as well as the overall care of the ship, their word is law, from a time for lights out to restrictions on fresh water usage and alcohol consumption.*

▶ *Ask the captain permission to come aboard. Think of the yachting experience as a vacation at the captain's luxury floating home where you are guest of honour. Asking permission to come aboard is the floating-home equivalent of knocking on a door.*

▶ *When you do board the yacht, take off your shoes to avoid damaging the carefully polished wood beneath your feet. Bring shoes with soft soles such as trainers or deck shoes – you will be expected to wear them onboard. If you use these shoes onshore, check their soles before using them on the yacht again.*

- ▶ *Don't waste fresh water as there will be a limited supply. If you have long hair, ask the captain or skipper whether there will be enough to wash it every day. It is far more important to have the fresh water to drink than for you to have a glossy head of hair.*
- ▶ *The toilet onboard often has a specific method of operation. Take care to follow the instructions as not doing so may result in a blockage.*
- ▶ *Keep noise levels down. When talking or listening to music or your television, consider whether anyone is asleep or relaxing quietly. Walls tend to be thin on yachts and sound carries easily so be mindful not only of whether you may be disturbing someone else, but also of what you are saying.*
- ▶ *If you want to look around the galley, ask permission from a crew member and let them suggest a time when it would be convenient as the galley can become particularly busy at certain times of the day, for example just before supper.*
- ▶ *Be careful not to drink too much on sailing holidays. A hangover combined with seasickness does not make a happy pairing. If you make friends onshore and your captain is still awake and in sight when you return, ask the captain's permission before bringing them aboard.*
- ▶ *Tip the crew upon leaving. It is best to hand the money to the captain in a sealed envelope with a suggestion on how to distribute it. It is customary to tip a total of between 10 and 15 per cent of the charter fee. Remember when leaving your instructions for distribution to include all those who have helped your stay to continue smoothly (for example, the navigation crew and dishwashers, not just the serving staff or those you have met personally). However, if your ideas for how to distribute the money are particularly uneven or do not include the captain, it is perhaps better to distribute sealed envelopes to the crew members individually.*

Etiquette abroad

Etiquette abroad is a tricky matter. Gestures and phrases can be wildly misinterpreted in different cultures. What you may think is perfect manners (a display of observation skills and consideration far beyond even what this book can offer) may go unnoticed or even deemed offensive by people of a different culture. For example, an 'okay' sign to the British is offensive to those in Brazil. You are unlikely to avoid every faux-pas of another culture every time you travel, but the tips below should make the process a little smoother.

▶ *When visiting a land with a language that you do not speak, buy a phrase book and learn a few key snippets such as 'please', 'thank you', 'good morning', 'where is…', and 'how much…'. Many foreigners believe English-speakers arrogant to assume their language is spoken across the globe. Learning a few simple phrases shows an understanding that this is not the case.*

▶ *Phrases such as 'good morning', 'good afternoon', 'good evening', 'please' and 'thank you' are often used far more liberally in non-British cultures, so use them frequently. A person is far less likely to think badly of you if you over-use these phrases than if you under-use them. If you have not managed to learn these phrases in the local language, say them in English and smile. Positive body language will get you far in a country where you don't speak the language.*

▶ *Don't insult or make fun of locals in your own native language, assuming that they will not understand. Apart from English being a somewhat universal language these days and the high risk that you are standing next to someone who can understand your potty mouth, it is simply bad manners to talk in this way and likely to cause offence as your shifty eyes and body language make the gist of what you are talking about obvious, if not the exact meaning.*

▶ *If travelling within the country, write down your destination on a piece of paper to show your taxi or bus driver if they do not understand your pronunciation of a place name.*

▶ *Be aware that what you may consider good manners in your home town may constitute a breach of etiquette in unfamiliar surroundings.*

▶ *Buy a guide book before you arrive. As well as equipping you with a little local knowledge that will grant you favour, a good quality guide book will tell you correct tipping practices in that country.*

▶ *When speaking to a local about their city or country, be complimentary, and never compare their city or country to your own unfavourably. Find something nice to say, even if it is just that the people are friendly, and then change the topic if your effusing on the wonders of their country is not genuine.*

▶ *Be cautious of using first names immediately. Use a title until invited to use a first name.*

▶ *Show interest in your surroundings. Ask questions about local customs as well as the tourist attractions – everyone likes to think that their own country is unique and interesting internationally. Avoid the topic of the politics of the country you are in, but be prepared to discuss your own country's politics and international involvement. Also avoid personal questions, such as those you would normally ask about family, as some find this line of questioning intrusive.*

▶ *Tell jokes with caution as they may not translate well to the culture, even if you are fluent in the language.*

▶ *Try not to balk at food or refuse foods or drinks that you are unused to. They were likely offered in kindness and should be accepted with a similar attitude.*

▶ *Mind your personal space. Different cultures have different ideas about what constitutes an invasion of personal space. Be aware that you may be intruding on someone else's, depending on their own ideas, so if they take a step back, take the hint and don't step forward.*

▶ *Use a guide book or an internet search to find out about general etiquette in the country you are visiting before you leave. Many of these sites highlight the differences in practice between Britain and the country you are visiting.*

▶ *Dress slightly conservatively and inconspicuously, keeping your shoulders covered, your skirts or shorts knee length or below and avoiding plunging necklines or transparent garments until you are sure that locals will not view more risqué attire styles as inappropriate. Be mindful that when visiting local attractions, in particular places of worship, that showing any flesh, even your calves and arms may be considered inappropriate. Check with a tour guide or with your hotel staff to find out what is acceptable.*

▶ *Check the rules about taking photographs before whisking out your camera and getting snap happy. In some places, such as museums and places of worship, using a flash camera is not permitted, and in others, taking photos at all is forbidden. Respect the rules, they are there to preserve the items which you are there to see and to encourage you to buy a souvenir postcard or photo, thus helping local trade and the maintenance of the place you have enjoyed.*

▶ *Being respectful with your camera includes not taking photos of the country's people without their permission, in particular children. In your own country you would expect a clout around the head for doing this and the same should apply for countries you are visiting. The inhabitants are not just figures for tourist interest; they are still human beings, even if their culture and way of life does fascinate you.*

▶ *Make an effort to see your actions through the eyes of the locals and act accordingly.*

▶ *Often, inadvertent breaches of etiquette will not be noticed by yourself, but if you do realize what you have done, say sorry immediately and try to explain yourself and the differences in culture using non-aggressive body language (for example, do not cross your arms) and perhaps make some gesture of goodwill such as offering to buy the offended person a drink before going your own way.*

Insight

Err on the side of formality when abroad until sure of the code of conduct. From attire choices to how to behave in public, it is easy to offend when you do not know the rules of society.

10 THINGS TO REMEMBER

1 *Be aware that etiquette abroad may be different to that of your own country. Make the effort to obey the rules of etiquette of other countries when visiting.*

2 *Make an effort to learn basic phrases in the language of the country you are visiting, such as 'hello', 'goodbye' and 'thank you'.*

3 *Keep your temper in cars, despite the bad driving of others.*

4 *Be organized with travel documents.*

5 *Obey weight limits set down by airlines for luggage.*

6 *Leave more than enough time for travelling and checking in where needed.*

7 *Be considerate of those you are travelling with. Take turns with music choices in cars; don't stand in the aisles to talk in planes; keep passion private.*

8 *If travelling with children, keep them entertained and don't let them disrupt others.*

9 *Respect the wishes of others not to be disturbed. If they obviously do not want to talk, leave them be.*

10 *Share and be mindful of not wasting resources that are scarce, whether that be suntan lotion or water.*

10

Dining etiquette

In this chapter you will learn how to:
- *use eating utensils*
- *behave at the table*
- *pay a dining bill*
- *eat a variety of difficult foods.*

Once seated, do not start eating until every person at your table has been served. However, at informal gatherings or if the service is poor, the host can and should indicate to those who have been served that they can start without contempt from other diners.

Place settings

Below are some general guidelines for how to use your eating utensils:

▶ *Etiquette for the use of a knife and fork differs from country to country. British etiquette states that when eating using a knife and fork, the knife is always held in the right hand and the fork is held in the left. The fork is held as shown in Figure 10.2, such that your index finger falls two-thirds of the way down the stem of the fork, and the knife such that your index finger falls just before the start of the blade.*

▶ *Hold glasses by the stem in order to avoid warming the liquid inside.*

- Eat pudding with the spoon using a fork, if provided, to push the food onto it.
- Use your knife and fork only to eat, not to gesticulate.
- If any piece of your cutlery drops onto the floor, ask for a replacement item.
- When you have finished with your knife and fork, place them together at either a 20-minutes-past the hour position or a half-past the hour position on your plate.

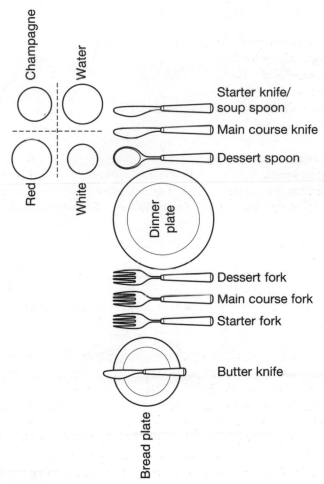

Figure 10.1 A complete place setting.

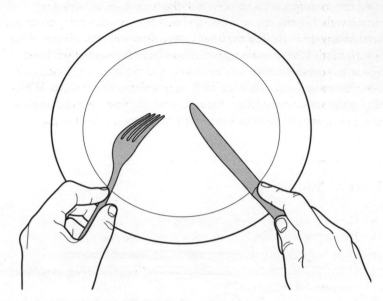

Figure 10.2 How to hold a knife and fork.

Eating soup

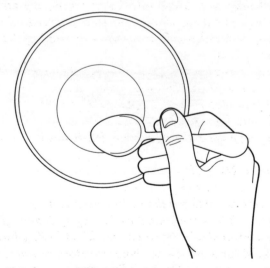

Figure 10.3 The correct way to hold a soup spoon.

Hold the soup spoon like a pen, with the handle touching your thumb web. Lift the spoon from the bowl by scooping away from you (so that any drips land in the bowl rather than your lap). When there is only a little soup remaining in the bowl, tilt the edge of the bowl closest to you away from you and again use the spoon to scoop in a direction away from you. Drink the soup quietly. Don't slurp. When resting the soup spoon leave it at a 20-minutes-past the hour angle in your bowl. When finished, leave it at a half-past the hour angle.

A list of 'don'ts'

▶ *Don't lean back on the hind legs of your chair.*
▶ *Don't put your arms over the back of the chair.*
▶ *Don't apply make-up or comb your hair at the table.*
▶ *Don't leave any personal items resting on the table, including your mobile phone.*
▶ *Don't take a call at the table. If you must keep your mobile phone on, leave it on vibrate in your pocket and take the call outside.*
▶ *Don't hold either your knife or fork while lifting a glass to drink. Instead, rest the knife and fork at a quarter-to-three or twenty-to-four position with the tines (prongs) of the fork facing downwards.*
▶ *Don't reach across another person for any item on the table – ask someone else to pass the object instead.*
▶ *Don't put your elbows on the table while you eat.*
▶ *Don't lick your knife or fork.*
▶ *Don't rearrange the cutlery if you are left-handed.*

ADDITIONAL NOTES

▶ *Red wine glasses are larger than white wine glasses. Champagne will be served in a flute (a longer, thinner glass).*
▶ *If you are presented with a fish knife (a blunt knife which has a fatter blade) for a fish course, hold your fork in your left hand as usual, and your fish knife like a spoon or pen.*

- ▶ When setting a table, the blade of a knife should always face left.
- ▶ The pudding spoon and fork may alternatively be placed at the top of the setting, above the plate and perpendicular to the other items of cutlery.
- ▶ Never add salt or pepper without tasting the dish first. If you feel that the dish requires a large addition of either, do so discreetly so as not to offend your host, particularly if they have cooked the meal themselves.
- ▶ If a lady leaves the table throughout a formal meal, men should rise off their seats (not fully stand) to acknowledge her leaving.
- ▶ Time your speed of eating such that you finish around the same time as everyone else at your table.
- ▶ Never double dip in sauces. If an item of food has made contact with your mouth, the food should not then touch a communal bowl of sauce.
- ▶ Don't lick your fingers. Use a napkin or finger bowl.

Insight

Remember that a dining table is a place for eating and enjoying eating with others. Concentrate on that task – doing so makes it easy for other to enjoy the meal. Also remember that if the person who cooked the food is present, they have spent time creating what you are eating so you should show due appreciation for the effort.

How to use chopsticks

Some foods and utensils of different cultures are so uncommon to the British that a lack of knowledge of how to use them is accepted, and the request of a knife and fork will not be met with rolled eyes. However, Chinese and Japanese food is now so frequently eaten in Britain that you should learn how to use chopsticks as a part of embracing these cultures.

1 With your right hand, hold the broad end of the first chopstick with your thumb web so that the thinner end rests between the ends of your middle finger and ring finger (see Figure 10.4). Throughout eating, this chopstick should stay steady and will not move.

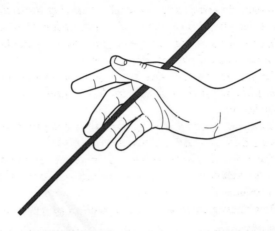

Figure 10.4.

2 Grip the second chopstick between your index finger and middle finger, like you would a pencil, with your thumb over the broad end (see Figure 10.5). Make sure the narrow tips of the chopsticks are even with each other to help you pinch the food and to prevent them from crossing.

Figure 10.5.

3 Hold the first chopstick still and move the second by moving the tip of your index finger up and down while the thumb remains relatively steady.

Figure 10.6.

Figure 10.7.

4 Practise opening and closing the chopsticks. Make sure the broad ends of the chopsticks do not cross as this will make it difficult to pick up food. Pick up food at any angle which creates stability – around 45 degrees is often best.

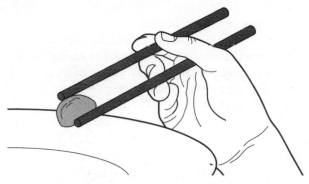

Figure 10.8.

Insight

Learning to eat with chopsticks can be difficult and at first, frustrating. But practise as much as you can at home, even with non-Asian food, and you will find it is easy to become skilful with them quickly.

OTHER CHOPSTICKS ETIQUETTE

- *Never lick your chopsticks.*
- *Hold your chopsticks in their middle or towards their broad end.*
- *Never stick your chopsticks into your rice straight down – this is bad manners because it resembles the incense burnt to mourn a dead relative in Chinese culture.*
- *Do not cross your chopsticks as this is a symbol of death.*
- *When you are finished with your chopsticks, lay them flat over your bowl or place them parallel back in your chopstick rest.*
- *The etiquette of different chopstick-using nationalities can vary from country to country. It is wise to check the etiquette of each before dining with someone from one of these countries.*

Insight

Using the culturally correct eating instruments for food enhances the experience of eating and absorbing other cultures.

Napkins

Upon arrival at the table, sit down and place the napkin over your lap. This gives the impression that you are ready to be served (if in a restaurant) or ready to eat (if in someone's home). Tucking the napkin into your shirt implies that you are to be eating with such little care that you expect to spill half your plate on yourself. Putting the napkin on your lap on the other hand, is a discreet way of catching the occasional crumb.

Use your napkin throughout the meal to dab at the corners of your mouth and remove stray crumbs or to wipe your hands. Never think that the edge of a tablecloth is a suitable alternative for either of these purposes. Don't use the napkin (or the tablecloth for that matter) to wipe your nose.

If at any point you leave the table during the meal, leave your napkin on your empty seat, not on the table. In a restaurant, if you drop your napkin on the floor, you should ask for another. In someone's home, on the other hand, it is rude to expect that the host will have a spare napkin, so don't ask. If, however, you are the host in this situation, you should offer a clean spare napkin if you have such an item available.

At the end of the meal, fold the napkin roughly and place to the left of your dining plate. Never leave a cloth napkin on the plate, particularly when dining at someone's house, and especially not if you are staying for more than one meal. It is rude to assume that the host has a plentiful supply of cloths which are suitable for a dining table, and thus the action of folding it and leaving it somewhere where it will not become additionally soiled implies that you would be willing to use the napkin for your next meal.

One last word on the subject of the cloth. If you are American, it is acceptable to say either 'serviette' or 'napkin'. If you are British and are eating in Britain, the word is 'napkin' and there is no other option.

Toothpicks

Although they are given to you at the table, they are not to be used there. If you must use a toothpick or have been eating a food which is likely to be caught in your teeth, such as spinach, take one of the toothpicks to the bathroom with you and use it there. Your hand is not enough of a shield to make this a polite thing to do at the table, and besides, where would you put it when you've finished covering it in pieces of half-chewed food extracted from between your teeth?

Wine

CHOOSING A WINE

In a restaurant, for a non-connoisseur, choosing a wine can be an unnecessarily difficult ordeal as, unlike your choice of food, everyone at the table will be forced to deal with the result of your choice, be it good or bad. These tips, however, should ensure that even if you inadvertently choose wine which tastes like battery acid, you do so with enough panache to ensure that the choice is bad luck rather than the obvious choice of a fool.

Typically, whoever did the inviting will pay (see page 154), so that person will also be expected to choose and taste the wine. If you are not comfortable in this role, simply delegate the responsibility to someone who is – either one of the guests present or the wine waiter.

White wine strictly with white meat and red strictly with red is no longer the hard and fast rule it once was as blends have become more complex and now a red can be lighter than a heavy white. The goal of the person saddled with the task of choosing a wine is to pair the food choices of the party with the choice of wine. Often the food choices are so varied that this would be impossible to do with one bottle. Consider ordering more than one bottle or ordering by the glass. Before looking at the wine menu, ask the party if they have any preferences. If the decision is left wide open to you, suggest a wine to the table before you order and ask whether your choice is acceptable to all. If you don't have a preference, ask the wine waiter to suggest a wine that complements your meals. If you know a little about wine, use your knowledge to make your questions specific, but keep it short – nobody likes a wine bore.

The most expensive wine is not always the best. In fact, if you are bluffing knowledge of grapes, it is a riskier choice than a mid-priced wine. You chance looking as though you have more money than sense should you choose the most expensive without good reason, be it sentimental or a matter of taste.

After ordering, the wine waiter will present your selection, label forward, to the person who has ordered the wine. This is quite simply to verify that it is the correct wine. Take care to check that it is indeed the right bottle and date rather than waiting to find at the billing time that you have unknowingly enjoyed a bottle at four times the expected price. The cork is removed and placed on the table – leave it there. Use the wine to decide whether the bottle is good.

A small amount will be poured for the host. Swirl the wine in the glass, smell and then taste.

Insight

Swirling of the wine is done to intensify the aromas. To avoid spillage, place the glass on the table and move it in circles around the size of a 5 p piece.

This is not an opportunity to reject a healthy wine on the grounds of taste preference, it is only to check that the wine has not been corked or spoiled in any other way.

Insight

Professional wine tasters spit wine out after trying it. In a restaurant though, swallow.

Corking is not, as many think, floating cork present in the glass as a result of poor corkscrew action. A wine is said to be corked when it has been in contact with a cork infected with a fungus that produces the chemical 1,2,4-trichloroanisole. It is this chemical (rather than the fungus itself) that gives the corked wine its unwelcome flavour. A spoiled wine is easy to spot, smelling as it does of gym socks and having a similar taste. There may also be unidentifiable floating objects or cloudiness.

If the waiter hands you the cork, it is for you to smell and touch to check for excess moisture, an indication that the wine may not have been stored properly. If you do not feel able to spot a spoiled wine from this ritual, there is no need to do it or to hand the cork around the table for someone else to check. It is far easier to decide whether a wine is spoiled from the sample poured for you.

After approval, the wine will be poured. Leave your glass on the table rather than trying to assist the server by lifting it towards them. It is much harder to hit a moving target. Depending upon the size of the glass, servers may pour as little as a quarter of a glass at a time. This is normal and not worthy of note. If you do not wish to drink, smile, look towards the server and say 'thank you but I'm not drinking.' Using your hand as a barrier or turning your glass upside down is seen as borderline dining aggressiveness. Red wine should be served at room temperature. Although ice buckets or coolers may not be automatically provided for white wine, do not be afraid to ask for one.

Throughout the meal, the waiter should return to top up your glasses. However, if the waiters are busy or just plain inattentive, feel free to do it yourself. In doing so, offer to refill the glasses of those sitting on either side of you first.

When the first order of wine has been finished, ask the table whether they are happy to continue drinking the same wine, or whether they would prefer you to choose another.

The drinking of champagne should be done before the start of the meal or at the end during any toasts. Drinking champagne throughout the meal is often considered flashy and in poor taste.

CORKAGE ETIQUETTE

Always call the restaurant in advance to verify that corkage is allowed and to ascertain the fee. Unless the restaurant is specifically advertised as one in which you bring your own wine, wine brought to a restaurant should be relatively rare or special in some way, and should never appear on the restaurant's wine list. After the waiter opens and pours the contents, it is polite to offer them a taste.

THE DUTY OF THE HOST AT HOME DINNER PARTIES

Before serving the wine, allow it time to breathe at room temperature. It is the host's responsibility to ensure discreetly that the wine is not spoiled. Give some thought to the order in which you want to open the wines if there is more than one type.

When pouring the wine, be aware of pouring sediment at the bottom of the bottle into a guest's glass and, if necessary, leave the last half glass of wine in the bottle.

Appropriate conversation topics

In this day and age, pretty much anything goes in terms of dining chatter apart from health issues (likely to provoke a loss of appetite); your dislike of the food (this is an insult to the host or the organizer); or politics and religion (a lively debate may well disintegrate into an all-out upsetting brawl). In addition, at business lunches, it is better if possible to leave talk of business until the plates for the first course have been cleared.

However, by far the rudest thing to talk about when eating is the subject of table manners and etiquette. Do not inform someone of his or her failings in this area. As far as table manners goes, this is much ruder than any possible slip of the fork.

How to complain

If you must complain, do it to the manager and do it without raising your voice. Even if the service was poor and the food vile, if you ate it, you should expect to pay for it.

Getting the attention of staff

If you click your fingers, say 'my man' or shrilly trill 'garçon', you are likely, and deserve, to have your food served up with whichever punishment the serving staff deem fit. The servers will have their eyes peeled for those who require assistance of some form. In the same way as you naturally do in a bar, try to catch the eye of one of the servers and perhaps, if you feel that further clarification is needed raise your hand, but to no higher than your eye level.

If you seem unable to catch the eye of one of the servers and attention is fairly urgently required, this is not an excuse to gesticulate wildly. Simply leave the table and go to a member of staff to explain that you require some service. Do it politely, there is no need to cause a scene. If you are unhappy with the service, show it in your lack of tip.

Champagne

Contrary to what most people believe, the polite way to open champagne is without a pop. To do this, remove the foil and wire casing. Hold the top of the cork with your left hand, placing the palm over the cork. Clasp and gently twist the bottle. Pour chilled champagne into flutes.

Difficult foods

Certain food have an etiquette all of their own. Some people consider grappling with lobster legs or carving an artichoke an extreme sport, to be taken on only by the vastly experienced and strong willed. Other foods are less fiddly but just as dangerous in terms of etiquette. The innocent looking lemon wedge, for example, has blinded many an unwitting diner. See below for some tips on how to tackle some of the trickier foods.

LOBSTER

If the lobster is still within its shell, you will need a nutcracker or mallet. Cocktail forks to remove the meat are also helpful.

Before the lobster is served, it will likely be cracked at all points with the tail split in half. Any cracking that you do yourself should be done with care, holding onto the lobster to be cracked and, when using a mallet, being attentive to the force of your swing. Do not stand up to use the mallet. Remember at all times that this is a civilized meal, not an iron man competition. Eat the tail meat by pulling out one piece at a time. There is much more meat to a lobster than just the claws and the tail, but you will need to crack open every piece to get at it, such as the legs. Good morsels can also be found under the animal's carapace, like the green 'tomalley' (digestive gland) and, in females, the red roe (unfertilized lobster eggs). If you pull out a particularly large piece, cut it with a knife and fork. The small claws can be cleaned and the meat sucked out, as if through a straw.

CRAB

As with lobster, you will need a mallet or nutcracker to open the shell if the chef has not prepared it in such a way so as to make it accessible with only a fork.

First, pull off the legs and claws as this is where the largest quantity of meat will be found. Next, crack open the shell, being careful not to splatter others. Most of what is inside the main part of the shell is edible but as body parts such as the lungs are contained within, it is often ignored.

Soft shell crab is cut and eaten as it is, with a knife and fork.

Because of the inevitable mess and time involved in eating a whole lobster or crab, it is advisable only to order it as a group. Many restaurants offer lobster or crab with the meat already removed from the shell. It may be ordered individually if it is served in this way. Use a bib if one is offered.

PRAWNS

When presented with a whole prawn, first remove the head. Hold the prawn with its legs facing upwards and peel away the shell starting between the middle of the legs and pulling along the width of the shell. Empty shell pieces should be placed into a separate waste bowl or on a separate plate.

OYSTERS

Insert your knife into the hinge at the back of the shell and prise open by cutting the hinge (some oysters are presented with a specific sturdy blunt knife for this purpose). Then, slide the knife underneath the meat and cut it away from the muscle which attaches it to the shell. Keep the oyster level so that the liquid inside does not spill. Using a twisting motion, pull the top and bottom shells apart.

Restaurants will likely serve oysters in a half shell, in which case simply run your knife between the shell and the oyster to ensure that it is loose, dress it with whichever condiment you prefer – hot pepper and lemon juice are the classic accompaniments – and drink the oyster out of the shell. Some people suggest chewing a raw oyster to fully appreciate the rich, salty taste, but it is easy and not poorly thought of to swallow an oyster in one gulp as many find the texture loathsome.

BREAD

On your bread plate, never cut bread with a knife, always break off bite-sized pieces and, if desired, apply butter. If the butter is on a shared plate, use the knife provided with it to move some onto your plate, and then use your own butter knife to butter the bread. Never dunk your bread in your soup.

SUSHI

Use chopsticks and/or fingers. Although some substitute a knife and fork for chopsticks to eat other Japanese or Chinese dishes, it is never acceptable to do this for sushi.

Sushi literally means 'with rice', but the term also refers to the dish of raw fish and rice-based pieces, which often includes rice and vegetables wrapped in a small seaweed roll with the fish. Once considered a rare Japanese delicacy, sushi is now commonplace in the western world even if the correct way of eating it is not.

First, pour some of the soy sauce into the small saucer provided. Too much soy sauce overpowers the delicate flavours of the fish, so to avoid the rice acting as a soy sauce sponge and also to prevent the rice from falling apart into the soy sauce bowl, nigiri (the sushi which is essentially a ball or rectangle of rice with a slice of fish on top) should be picked up with fingers, turned over so that the fish is facing downward and then dipped into the soy sauce. The nigiri should then be eaten fish side down, so that the flavour of the fish is the first to reach the taste buds.

In general, when eating any type of sushi, remember that soy sauce is not a necessary component of the meal and should be used sparingly. Some forego the soy sauce entirely. Where possible, avoid dunking the majority of the rice into the soy sauce. Nigiri should be eaten in one bite. Sushi rolls with seaweed on the outside should be eaten first from a platter as the seaweed can become soggy.

Sashimi (slices of raw fish without rice) should be eaten with chopsticks. Using your chopsticks, a little wasabi (green Japanese horseradish) should be placed on one corner of the fish. Another corner of the fish should be dipped into the soy sauce. Wasabi is very peppery. Use tiny amounts unless you enjoy the sensation of snorting fire. Some think that wasabi should not be added to soy sauce as contact with liquid removes the flavour of the wasabi, but it is not generally considered an etiquette faux pas to do so as this behaviour is common among both Japanese and Westerners.

For traditional sushi rolls and nigiri, the wasabi has usually been carefully added by the chef between the fish and the rice with the same consideration that a British chef would give to the use of salt to balance flavours. More can be added to taste, but be mindful that the strong flavour of the wasabi is thought to be used in less reputable establishments to mask the taste of low-quality fish. As such, at a sushi bar, it is better to tell the chef that you prefer more wasabi and let him or her incorporate it in your dish. If you are at a table and would prefer to add it yourself, do so sparingly.

To cleanse your palate between different types of sushi, chew and eat a piece of the pickled ginger. Some sushi restaurants or bars provide each customer with a damp cloth. If eating with your fingers, use the cloth to wipe your hands between sushi pieces in order to keep the flavours separate.

Sake, beer or green tea are thought to be the best beverages to drink when eating sushi. Many believe wine to have too strong a flavour to complement the sushi.

SHISH KABOB

Holding the shish kabob in one hand, use a fork to remove the pieces with the other. Apply pressure, but not so much that the food will go flying should the piece suddenly move unexpectedly. For pieces that seem stuck, simply continue applying the pressure for longer and the piece will eventually give. After all the food is transferred from the skewer to your plate, place the skewer on the side of the plate. Eat the pieces removed using a knife and fork.

DONNER KEBAB AT 4.00 A.M. AS YOU LEAVE A CLUB

Hold with both hands and use a napkin. Lean forward so as to not let the chilli sauce or mayonnaise spill down your clothing. Do not under any circumstances eat any part of your kebab which has dropped on the floor. There are no exceptions to this, including the three-second rule. Share with other hungry, alcohol-fuelled friends. If you are joining someone in bed at home, make sure to brush your teeth particularly vigorously.

ESCARGOTS (SNAILS)

You will need an escargot tong and a cocktail fork. Using the escargot tong, pick up one escargot at a time. Remove the snail from its shell using the cocktail fork and dip into sauce if available. Put the shell into a separate bowl. The butter sauce may be delicious but this is no excuse to lick the shell.

FAJITAS

Do not overfill. Use the serving spoons provided to load your wrap, but use your hands to wrap the fillings in. If the fillings are shared, take care to take only your share of each so as not to leave the last person with no guacamole. Take care to secure the end furthest from your mouth – a task which is made easier if you have been restrained in your filling habits. Lean over the plate to eat, but not down onto it. The fillings may fall onto the plate. When this happens, use a knife and fork and not your fingers to eat it.

CHEESE

If the cheese is presented as a sector from a round, cut pieces lengthways as the nose of the cheese (the centre point) is richer than the edge.

If the cheese is a hard cheese presented in a square, cut any which way you like.

ARTICHOKES

Artichoke leaves are consumed using only the fingers. The heart of the artichoke is eaten with a knife and fork. Remove one leaf at a time. Holding the thin top end of the artichoke leaf, dip the thicker base of the leaf into the sauce provided. Still holding the less thick end of the artichoke, pull the leaf between your teeth, removing and eating the fleshy part of the leaf. You do not eat the rest of the leaf. Put it to the side of your plate or on another plate, if available. After removing and eating all the large leaves, you will find some small purple-ish leaves with sharp points at the top. Remove these and do not eat. You will now be left with the artichoke heart. Cut into bitesize pieces using a knife and fork and use your fork to dip the artichoke into the sauce.

GRAPES

Use grape shears (if available) or fingers to cut or break a branch of grapes off the main cluster and place on your plate. From the bunch you have taken, remove the grapes individually by hand.

Seeded grapes can be eaten by either cutting into the grape with a fruit knife and removing the seeds, or by eating the grapes whole and removing the seeds from your mouth with your fingers. Never place removed seeds onto the main platter of fruit; either put them on your own plate or onto a napkin.

MELON

In a restaurant or at a formal dinner, if the melon is served cut in half, use a spoon to scoop the flesh away from the skin. If the wedge is thin, the melon can be eaten with a knife and fork. If the melon has been presented in cubes, use a fork, not a spoon.

Watermelon is usually served in a wedge and should be eaten with a knife and a fork if seated and presented with cutlery. Extract the seeds with the knife and fork. In an informal setting, melons can be eaten without cutlery, but try to remove the seeds as best you can first or take the seeds from your mouth using your thumb and forefinger. In company, never spit the seeds, even if outdoors, unless you are in a jungle or other such remote place and have no means by which to clean your hands.

CHERRY TOMATOES

As a canapé, always eat whole. On a plate, gently prick the skin with a fork and eat whole or cut in half carefully. Never stab the cherry tomato as it may produce an unexpected spurt.

SPAGHETTI

The traditional way of eating spaghetti states that one should scoop a few strands of spaghetti with a fork, put the tines of the fork onto a part of the plate which does not contain spaghetti and twirl these withdrawn strands into a neat nest which is then popped into the mouth. Purists believe that spaghetti and noodles should not be cut with a knife or spoon as the strands represent longevity. The modern lady or gentlemen knows that it is damned fiddly stuff and any way to get it from your plate to your mouth with minimum mess is fair play. Try to minimize cutting if possible but feel free to use your spoon as a guide, making the creation of a mini-spaghetti nest that little bit easier. The only rule which remains is this: if, upon reaching your mouth some strands of spaghetti are dangling out in a bird-with-a-worm fashion, bite and let the pieces fall back to the plate if necessary. Do not suck the strands up into your mouth unless you are trying to create some sort of modern art piece with your clothing and pasta sauce. And only tuck a napkin into your shirt if you are under the age of five.

PEAS

Keeping peas on the back of your fork without the right technique is akin to nailing jelly to a wall. These days some think it reasonable to turn your fork over and use it as a shovel for your peas. There are others, however, who find this fork-as-a-spoon trick still entirely reprehensible, so as frustrating as it may be, it is advisable when you are in unfamiliar company to mind your peas. With your fork in your left hand and the prongs turned down, use another part of the meal to create a backstop on the fork. Scoop a few peas up onto the back of the fork and carefully lift to your mouth. This is a trick most easily accomplished when the other part of the dish is something tacky, such as mashed potato. Although you should endeavour not to leave yourself in such a situation, if only peas remain on your plate, stab a few of your peas onto the tines of your fork and scoop others onto the back of the fork. The pronged peas should keep the others in place. Do not mash your peas in order to overcome the pea problem.

MUSSELS

Eat only open mussels. Use either a cocktail fork or the hinged empty shell of another mussel as pincers to remove other mussels from their shells. Eat the extracted mussel whole. Make plentiful use of the bowl of water provided to wash your fingertips throughout the meal, for example, between eating a mussel and raising your wine glass.

OLIVES

In a formal setting, when olives are served on a condiment or relish tray, use an olive fork or stick if provided to place them on your plate. From that point, olives are considered a finger food. In an informal setting it is fine to eat the olives straight from the bowl, but once an olive has been touched with the fingers, it should be eaten or discarded, never left in the shared bowl. If the olives contain stones, put the whole olive in your mouth and remove the stone using your first finger and thumb. Put the stone in a separate bowl provided specifically for this purpose, in a napkin or on the side of your plate – never back in the shared bowl.

ORANGES

In a formal setting use the fruit knife to remove both ends and then the rind. Cut into quarters or pull off segments using your fingers. Rind on easier to peel citrus fruits, such as satsumas, can be removed using the fingers and the fruit should be broken into segments using your fingers, rather than cut using a knife.

LEMON WEDGES

Secure the lemon wedge with a fork and squeeze away from other people. If a fork is not available, use one hand to squeeze the wedge and the other to shield yourself and others from stray squirting.

CHIPS

Chips in a formal setting should be eaten with a knife and fork, whereas in an informal setting, they are considered a finger food. Use of the wooden spear offered for chip shop chips is strictly optional.

BURGERS

In a formal setting, burgers should be cut in half. Each half may then be picked up individually and eaten as you would a sandwich. Lean forward to ensure that any filling from the burger that drops out lands on the plate. This filling may be eaten later with a knife and fork. In more informal settings, pick the whole burger up to eat.

BARBEQUES

Hot dogs, hamburgers, ribs and small chicken pieces are treated as finger foods. To eat steak, fish and large chicken pieces, use a knife and fork, cutting one bite at a time.

CHICKEN

In a formal setting, chicken is always eaten with a knife and fork, no matter which cut you are served.

CORN ON THE COB

In a formal setting, remove the corn from the cob with a steak knife and eat using a fork. Informally, eat the corn on the cob by holding with both hands and using your teeth.

BANANA

At a formal dinner, peel the banana, place the peel on the side of the fruit plate, cut it into bite-size pieces using the fruit knife and eat pieces using the fruit fork. Informally, if you don't know how to eat a banana you are unlikely to be old enough to be able to read this explanation.

Trying new foods

Only do this among friends, never at business lunches or at formal events where you do not know all the guests well. Explain your predicament and hopefully someone will show you the way. If nobody knows the correct way to eat a food then take heart in that it will be difficult to offend them. Ask the serving staff for rough guidelines on which parts are edible and inedible, then dig in.

Canapés

Try to avoid foods that may get messy. Think about their size as well as their texture. If you do attempt them, have a napkin ready to deal with flying pieces or dripping sauce. If you end up with something in your mouth that you cannot chew, discreetly transfer it from your mouth to your napkin and dispose of it in the restroom or on the tray for the used plates and glasses.

Invasion of personal space

Although table manners are often considered the trickiest part of etiquette because of all the extra tools involved, peaceful eating at the table can be achieved by observing similar ground rules for polite day-to-day living. Think about how you can help those who need it and how to avoid the invasion of someone else's personal space. Even if you hold your fork like an ape and drink champagne out of a mug, provided you find a way in which to do so without jutting your elbow into someone else's face, it is likely that no one will balk at your breach of the finer points.

Paying

Whoever does the inviting does the paying. Others should not order the most expensive item on the menu. If, however, there is no obvious host, the bill should be split equally. Adding the cost of specific meals and drinks is crass as it displays a lack of generosity and far too much time is expended on talk of money, which is not the most pleasant topic of conversation to end an enjoyable supper. If splitting the bill, try to remember to bring cash as it makes the process considerably less painful for both you and the serving staff. If, however, it is clear that some have ordered particularly frugally, not drinking alcoholic beverages, for example, then it falls to the others to insist upon paying more. But take a generous guess at what the division should be rather than calculating exactly and throw in an extra note.

As unjust as it may seem, those who earn significantly more should pay more, without making a grand show of it. If you are a big earner, throw an extra note in claiming that you had more wine than everyone else or a more expensive dish. Eating out is an expensive business and the extra few pounds may make all the difference to those on a tight budget. Feel the glow of generosity and remember that it is easier for a camel to pass through the eye of a needle than for a rich man to enter the kingdom of heaven... but if you pay more than your fair share at the last supper, you'll likely be invited back and offered the extra big needle and miniature camel.

10 THINGS TO REMEMBER

1 *Whoever is paying should choose the wine. If this person feels unable to choose well, they should delegate the task.*

2 *Don't use toothpicks at the table.*

3 *Take note of how to use a knife and fork.*

4 *Wait until everyone has been served before starting to eat.*

5 *Complain quietly in restaurants.*

6 *Never click your fingers to get the attention of serving staff.*

7 *Eat difficult foods carefully, making an effort not to squirt other diners with your food.*

8 *Whoever does the inviting does the paying.*

9 *Keep your elbows in and don't reach or talk across others. Avoid invading the personal space of other people around the dining table.*

10 *If splitting the bill, do so evenly.*

11

Public speaking

In this chapter you will learn how to:
- *choose your phrases for speaking in public*
- *choose your subject matter*
- *make toasts, introductions, thank yous, presentations and main speeches*
- *speak on radio or television.*

General pointers for public speaking

Insight

Look in the mirror before speaking in public. Make sure your hair is in place and there's no food in your teeth. If you look good, you will feel confident when speaking.

USING A MICROPHONE

If possible, arrive early to test the microphone. Once speaking, judge your volume from the faces of your audience and adjust your position or voice projection if necessary to decrease or increase the volume. Having made this volume adjustment, keep still. If the microphone seems to be causing more problems than it is solving, try to make do without it and project your voice instead.

AVOID CLICHÉS

If the phrase is one that you are used to hearing or seeing written down, it will bore people if you say it.

USE OF STATISTICS

Statistics can be a valuable tool in strengthening your argument but they are not absorbed well aurally. Keep them to a vital few and, where possible, don't use numbers to present your statistics. For example, instead of 50 per cent, say 'a half'; for 51 per cent say 'just over a half'.

USING HUMOUR

Speeches can be made snappier, lighter and more entertaining by the careful application of humour. However, for it to work the humour must be relevant and flow well into the speech. As convenient as it may be to provide humour at the expense of someone else's dignity, don't.

SWEARING

Never swear. In your head it may sound funny or dramatic but out loud it will likely just sound crude, and you risk offending the more delicate members of your audience.

Toasts

MAKING A TOAST

You may be provided with some warning that you will be asked to give a toast, but equally, you may also be asked to provide words out of thin air with only a few minutes' notice. Try to remember that the purpose of a toast is to present the person being toasted in a favourable light. If you have been asked to toast, the chances are that you know the person well enough to do this.

If you have been given little notice, which is often the case, don't panic. While everyone's glasses are being filled, think about the person being toasted, what is special about them and of the fun times that you have spent together or activities in which they are known to participate.

To get the attention of the group, stand, holding your glass in the air (do not tap your glass). Put your glass down and talk slowly, clearly and sincerely about the person you have been asked to toast.

Insight

When toasting someone, stand facing them and make regular eye contact. Towards the end of your toast, sweep the room once with your eyes to include the audience.

Talk about the person in the third person and speak for the group, for example, 'I think we can all agree that Julia is normally the life and soul of the party but the time in Spain when she started a four-day relay siesta with the locals was perhaps her finest hour'. Most toasts are given at light-hearted events, so be light-hearted in your wording.

Speak for between one and three minutes bathing the toastee in a complimentary light, even if the angle you must take is that their friends still adore them despite a host of named not-so-serious faults. This is not an opportunity to embarrass anyone – keep the toast clean, particularly if children or the toastee's parents are present. Don't use in-jokes that some people at the event will not understand.

Finish with, 'Please stand and join me in raising a glass to [person's name]', raise your glass, sip and sit down. If in a restaurant, it is better to omit the standing.

DUTIES OF THE PERSON TOASTED

If you are the person receiving the toast, stay seated and do not drink. Standing or sipping will seem as though you are congratulating yourself. However, the person being toasted should consider standing and responding to the toast when it is finished, thanking both the person who made the toast and the host. If the toast is not directed at a particular person but is meant for everyone in the room, for example, patriotic toasts or toasting a sports team, everyone can join in the drinking.

WHAT TO DRINK

Champagne or wine are traditional for making toasts, but non-alcoholic beverages such as water, juice and soda are good substitutes for those not drinking. For informal settings, toast with any beverage you like.

LOYAL AND PATRIOTIC TOASTS

Loyal toasts are those to the reigning monarch. It requires just one sentence: 'Ladies and gentlemen, the Queen.' All should stand.

Patriotic toasts are those to the military services. Like loyal toasts, they are simple: stand, say 'To her majesty's forces', raise your glass, sip and sit.

If you are in the audience of the toast, unless instructed otherwise, you rise for the duration of the final words of the toast, raise your glass with the toaster, sip and then sit again. The corresponding response to any toast is to say '[the toastee's name]', sip and sit.

Introductions

Before making public introductions, do your research. To make an introduction you will need to present the person who is to speak, giving their name and their qualification for speaking. Make sure that you can pronounce the names of those you are introducing correctly, that you have checked their title and have confirmed without a doubt their background, why they are speaking and the topic they will be speaking on. Traditional introductions finish with the name of the person you are introducing, in the form, 'Ladies and gentlemen: John Doe'.

Keep the introduction short and specific – the audience is there to hear the main speaker, not a rambling introduction. If you are in the audience, at the end of the introduction clap to indicate your agreement that this is a worthy speaker.

Main speakers

BASICS

▶ *If you were introduced, always thank that speaker.*
▶ *Look at your listeners, making eye contact with as many as you can and speaking to them rather than at them.*
▶ *Do not exceed a time limit if there is one. Always aim to finish your speech earlier than expected rather than later.*
▶ *Make a concerted effort not to bore your audience. Structure your speech well. Start with something surprising to grab their attention and finish with a dramatic flair. Practise.*
▶ *Use notes to remind you of the key points of your speech, rather than memorizing or reading the whole speech. This way it will sound more natural, like a conversation with a group of people, and less like a lecture.*
▶ *Be sincere and do your research. It is rude to expect people to listen to you if you have no depth of knowledge about the subject on which you are speaking*

ASSESS YOUR AUDIENCE

Consider who you will be speaking to and adapt your speech appropriately. Use words that you think will be understood; don't use jargon, acronyms or colloquialisms unless you are sure that the audience will be familiar and comfortable with their use. Choose words appropriate for your audience.

However, with this in mind, don't speak down to your audience, particularly to the elderly or the young. Neither of these groups is stupid – as long as you adjust your speech to make it accessible to them, the subject matter should still be understandable. You may be more of an authority on the matter about which you are speaking, but your audience members would like to be treated as intelligent human beings.

Insight

People without confidence in public speaking tend to fall into the trap of apologizing for their speech. Don't, unless you're apologizing for something specific, for example if you are late, as it will only draw attention to any small errors which may otherwise go unnoticed.

AVOID TANGENTS

Whatever the subject of your speech, stay on topic. The audience has committed their time to listen to a speech on a certain subject and movements away from this topic will not be appreciated, even for non-business speeches. For example, if you are speaking at a wedding, stay on the subject of the bride, groom and experiences of the two, without branching off to recall who won the Champion's League the year they met and how you remember that because you met your own girlfriend that year and how exactly you two met, complete with tales of your first date and continuing relationship.

Making a presentation

If you were introduced by someone, you must first thank them. If you are making a presentation, it also falls to you to praise the event's organizers and the standard of the other contestants if there was competition for the award. It is normal to also explain why the presentation is being made and then name the winner with the words 'It is my pleasure to present this award to...', or words to that effect.

Accepting an award

Smile, look pleased and make your speech brief. Say thank you to the committee that has given you the award, as well as anyone who has helped you in attaining the award (coaches, parents, etc.). Prepare for the award ceremony by thinking through what you will say if you win the award. If the list of those you need to thank is long, write it down and take it with you to refer to when you make your acceptance. Don't cut the list unless saying the list of names takes more than two minutes (this will accommodate roughly 100 names) – it is far better to thank ten people who did not expect the gratitude than to forget one person who did and deserved it.

Vote of thanks

The vote of thanks used to be a formal affair requiring an intricately prepared speech, but these days it is more likely to be a spontaneous matter. The key to giving a good vote of thanks is to listen to the main speaker and show in your thanks that you have absorbed what the speaker has said.

Do not argue with or correct points made within the main speech. If you are tempted to do either of these or if the main speech greatly differed from your own thoughts and principles, use a phrase such as 'Thank you Mr Smith for a controversial speech that I am sure will keep us all thinking for a while'. Finish with, 'Ladies and gentlemen, please join me in showing your appreciation for [insert name]'.

Speaking on the radio or on television

If you are unqualified to speak on the topic proposed, turn down the invitation and, if possible, suggest someone in a better position to comment. If you have been chosen to represent an organization or committee, check before accepting that the organization or committee are happy to have the topic discussed and to have you as their representative. Ask why you have been chosen to appear and make your judgement from that.

Consider asking for a list of questions before the interview. This will give you an opportunity to think about what you want to answer, but don't rehearse precise responses as this will ruin the flow. Keep answers to more than one word but short and unwieldy. Don't repeat yourself but keep strictly to the point. Concentrate on speaking slowly and clearly and keeping 'ums' to a minimum. Practise with a friend before the appearance. Don't swear, and do think seriously about whether any joke you make could be offensive to anyone listening.

Time will be in short supply. Obey the studio presenter's or producer's instructions on when to wrap up what you are saying. For television, dress neatly and appropriately.

10 THINGS TO REMEMBER

1 *Don't swear while public speaking.*

2 *Arrive early to test the microphone.*

3 *Keep statistics to a minimum.*

4 *Use humour, but be careful to keep it relevant, non-embarrassing and accessible to the whole audience.*

5 *Stand when toasting and keep the toast short and full of good sentiment.*

6 *If the toast is to one person, the subject of the toast should not drink.*

7 *Do as much research as possible on your chosen subject and expect questions.*

8 *Avoid tangents off the theme of your speech.*

9 *Speak with language accessible to your chosen audience.*

10 *When accepting an award, thank as many people as have helped you achieve it.*

12

City survival

In this chapter you will learn how to:
- *survive in crowds*
- *use city transport*
- *cope with day-to-day city life.*

The practice of etiquette, for much of the time, is carried out in order to fit in. However, in the city, the trouble with this is that there are those people who consider quite rude behaviour a way of life. So what are the tricks to behaving well?

In cities, personal space is the size of a matchbox, strangers seem more threatening and there are simply more people to be aware of offending. There are few hard and fast rules that will substitute for observance and consideration towards others, but those given below outline some of the most common errors.

Walking speed

City folk want to get everywhere fast. Who knows why that man in the suit chose to sprint the mile to the tube rather than leave the house five minutes earlier, or whether that woman with the stroller is in fact training for a marathon. The city fascination with walking fast is less a necessity and more a way of life, but in entering a city you enter an agreement to keep up – or at least to try not to get in the way. Step up the pace if you can and walk in straight lines where possible. Swerving over the pavement looks ungainly and also obstructs others. Use the body language of someone in control – walk tall with your head held high and allow your peripheral vision to guide your next step. Do not stand in the middle of the pavement to look at a map, stand at the edge.

For those already trying to break the land speed record on foot, remember that despite a habitual anxiety to reach the tube station three minutes earlier, it is simply not morally sound to fell three elderly ladies and stand on a child.

Navigating a busy city is difficult. Before we are allowed to drive, we need to pass tests to demonstrate courteous and safe behaviour when dealing with others on the road. The traffic on the pavement is often much more tricky, but our only guidance is the practice of etiquette as described above.

STROLLERS

Surviving labour does not mean you own the pavement. Do not bash strollers into the ankles of others. In addition, do not nudge the stroller into the road as a method of slowing traffic – it is perilous for the child in your care and rudely puts yourself before the right of way of the road.

Crossing roads

Look before you cross the road and don't step out in front of cars. It is bad manners to be run over and not be around to identify the fault as your own. If a car stops to let you pass, raise your hand to breastbone height in thanks as you cross, even if it was on a pedestrian crossing.

Mind your bags

Donkeys can look graceful compared to many die-hard
shoppers at the end of a gruelling Saturday afternoon on
Oxford Street. Others may just have the one bag and the grace
of a gazelle but feel the need to twirl their new shoes with glee
at the end of one fingertip. Neither of these postures is ideal
for crowded spaces such as those encountered in a city. Most
understand that large numbers of bags are difficult to carry and
will not begrudge a little more space for the enthusiastic shopper.
In turn, the enthusiastic shopper should take care to be mindful
that their bags do not create a veritable assault course for others.
Ensure that bags are kept close to your side – knock your own leg
in preference to a stranger's if the need arises. It's your shopping,
after all.

Be considerate when resting your bags. Where possible, do not
leave them where a stranger will need to step around them. If you
have a vast number of bags, try not to travel on public transport
during rush hour – if time allows, stop at a café until the busy
time passes.

Escalators and elevators

On escalators, stand on the right with bags in front of or behind
you, and walk on the left. Non-compliance leaves others to
assume one of two things – either you are rude or have not passed
formative years in the developed world.

Elevators, although created to prevent people getting hot under
the collar, often do just that as we start to take them for granted.
Where possible, use the stairs to go up or down two flights of stairs
in order to prevent a possibly already crowded lift from stopping
for you.

Be particularly mindful of whether you need to use a lift
rather than the stairs at busy times of the day such as the
start of work, lunchtime and at the end of the working day.

On both elevators and escalators, give way to those who are
struggling with luggage and offer your help. Always hold the
doors for people who look as though they intend to enter unless
the elevator is already full to capacity.

The underground and buses

Here are a few guidelines:

▶ *Be aware of who is sitting and who is standing. Never be
embarrassed to offer your seat to another person you feel
may be more in need of it. Stories of well-meaning gentlemen
being knocked out by elderly women taking offence abound,
but remember that in these situations the elderly woman will
have been seen as the badly mannered party in the affair by
the surrounding people.*

▶ *Both men and women should be prepared to offer their seats
to elderly people or pregnant women, but men should jump to
do this whereas a woman should do it without complaint only
if it seems that none of the men has the intention of rising. It is
not etiquette law that men should give up their seats to similar-
aged women, but doing so will mark you out as an exceptional
gentleman for understanding the agony of high heels.*

▶ *Women – do not feel affronted if men do not (or do) offer you
a seat, but feel free to curse in your mind (not out loud) any
man who races to a seat against you, gets there at about the
same time and sits down with a satisfied grunt of contentment.*

▶ *If you are with a child under the age of five and seats are
scarce, put the child on your lap rather than leaving them to
occupy a seat which could be used by a fully grown person.*

- *Never leave your bags on an otherwise vacant seat when the tube is crowded and seats are sparse. Put them on your lap or on the floor.*
- *You may ask a person to move their bags if they are occupying a seat that you want to sit in; you may not ask a person to move their child.*
- *As polite as it is to hold a door open for a friend to enter a building or room, don't hold the tube door open, particularly in rush hour. Wait for the next tube. Holding the door open delays perhaps 500 people for 30 seconds (in other words, causes a total time delay of around four hours), whereas waiting for the next tube will take about two minutes, sometimes one.*
- *If you are standing near the door when the tube is crowded, step off the train to let others off and then re-board.*
- *It may be crowded, but do not push. Two bodies cannot occupy the same space at the same time.*
- *In rush hour, only open your newspaper if the space exists to do so without brushing it against others. If this is not possible, content yourself with reading the folded outside pages.*
- *Smile at strangers on public transport, but do not talk. If you think you may have seen the love of your life, pass the object of your affection a card or a slip of paper with your number as either you or she disembarks. Do not ask for their number; do not attempt to engage them in conversation.*

HYGIENE

Being clean and tidy is not merely a matter of personal pride but also of respect to others. Use deodorant and brush your teeth. Wear clean clothes. Horrid smells are particularly noticeable in small spaces. Shower in the morning every day, particularly in the summer.

Paying for shopping

Be courteous but brief at the cashier for the sake of the cashier and the queue behind. In crowded coffee shops, fast food joints or places with a long queue, pay with cash where possible. Try not to use large notes for small payments, particularly at market stalls where a ready supply of small notes and coins is often unavailable, but apologize if it is unavoidable. If you are the vendor and this happens, understand that it is unavoidable and, chin up, don't mention it and maybe the next guy will pay entirely with 5p pieces.

Insight

Don't forget to take the earphones of your MP3 player out and finish your mobile phone conversation before dealing with the cashier.

At the ATM

For many, the fear of withdrawing your last ten pound note of the month only to have it wrenched from your grip by the person behind you is enough to heighten the senses to all within an arm's distance. Others hide their PIN number as they would their answers to a spelling test in pre-school exams, with regular surreptitious glances over each shoulder. The trouble is that common thieves these days often do not obey the traditional dress code of a balaclava and gangster gear, and thus the average city dweller finds it harder to differentiate between a true criminal and an average Joe with personal space issues. To mark yourself as a kindly, non-prison bound sort, stand well back, (about two metres if you can) while looking in the direction of the ATM to make it clear that you are in the queue. Focus on anything in that direction except the number pad. And don't wear a balaclava.

Taxis

Being an inoffensive taxi client is just as important as the driver being courteous. Remember that it is often the driver's own car so you should treat it with the same respect as you would treat your own – don't slam the door or bring excess mud in on your shoes. Do tip the driver (see page 224). But on no account call him 'Mr Taxi Man' or 'driver' as it is condescending. For the taxi driver, the phrase 'time is money' has never been more true. Get the money ready to be handed over before the end of the ride.

AND FINALLY...

Crime
Rates of crime are higher in the city than elsewhere. If someone mugs you, many will understand you forgetting some of the finer points of etiquette. If your bag is snatched and you are fortunate enough to catch the criminal at fault, feel free to bounce your bags (and palm) against them as you leave, and ignore any restrictions on swearing. Call them what you like, they'll be expecting it, provided children aren't near, naturally.

Strip club etiquette
Obey the house rules. If you feel that at some point you have broken or bent one of these rules and in some way annoyed or offended the staff, tip well to avoid bad feeling. At all points when deciding how much to tip, consider how much you would charge to do the same job and be generous.

10 THINGS TO REMEMBER

1 *Be mindful of others in a rush and be mindful of others when you are in a rush.*

2 *Keep strollers out of the way where possible.*

3 *Stop your bags bashing into others.*

4 *Give way to those with luggage in crowded lifts and on escalators.*

5 *Walk up or down two flights of stairs at times of day when the lift is likely to be busy.*

6 *Give your seat on public transport to those who need it more than you.*

7 *Put small children on your lap, not their own seat, on crowded public transport.*

8 *Smile at strangers on public transport but do not insist upon conversation if it seems unwelcome.*

9 *Treat cabs with the respect with which you would treat your own car.*

10 *Do not put bags on public transport seats when seats are limited.*

13

Relationship etiquette

In this chapter you will learn how to:
- *chat up a prospective partner*
- *date*
- *juggle friends and family together with your relationship*
- *finish the relationship.*

Evolutionists claim the practice of etiquette is an activity created in the same manner as symmetrical faces, wide hips and big breasts on women and tall, chiselled features on men. They say the sole purpose of etiquette stems from a desire to find a worthy mate with whom to reproduce; it is a sign of good breeding, good parentage and thus good genes. As such, it is no wonder that relationship etiquette and manners for sexual purposes are forefront in the minds of men and women today, and treatment of the opposite sex seems for many the most important aspect of manners in any age. In the days of yesteryear, the most prominent aspects of etiquette were those involving relations with the opposite sex – introductions, courting and marriage proposals to name but a few. The core purpose of etiquette remains the same – the metaphorical peacock's feather to attract a mate – but the rules have drastically altered even over the last 50 years.

The guidelines for behaviour listed below apply to sexual relationships, be they heterosexual or homosexual. For liberated but less scientific minds, the final result of childbirth is not so important these days as the day-to-day find of someone to roll around in bed with. In addition to this alteration from the norm of 50 years ago, feminism, although it has undoubtedly had its benefits, has troubled the world of etiquette. With the liberalization of the fairer sex has come a plethora of difficulties in setting out the 'right' way to treat members of the opposite gender. Men want to be generous and women do not want to relinquish equality and the right to burn their bra if it takes their fancy later on in the evening. Following the rules of etiquette as below enacts a book of rules rather than a judgement on the capability of the sexes.

First principles

General tips:

- *Men and women can now both request a date. However, when asking, avoid staring at breasts or genitalia.*
- *Mind your invasion of your quarry's personal space. Keeping someone at arm's length until they decide on you is more likely to bring them closer later on.*
- *Cheesy chat-up lines are woefully inadequate and display a lack of originality. Potential partners like to think that they are special and uniquely fabulous to the wooer. Using a tired line implies that this is in fact not the case. If the line can be delivered with heavy irony, it may grant a brief window in which to charm, by adding a layer of unrivalled wit and interesting, thoughtful conversation, but the going may be tough. Women are most likely to be able to pull this off when approaching a man as they also have a traditional role-reversal novelty factor on their side.*
- *For a less perilous self-introduction, men and women can offer to buy each other drinks. However, the drink does not purchase the buyer time with the recipient – that is for the recipient of the drink to consider independently. It is rude, nonetheless, not to say thank you after the first drink and to accept more than one of these proffered beverages without having a conversation with the buyer. Upon being offered a*

third, if the intention of the buyer is obviously romance, the recipient should not accept unless they share the same feelings. No matter how broke you are, never ask for the cash instead.

▶ Alternatively, think of something original to say and start with that. Being funny helps but you don't have to be Ricky Gervais to come up with something unique, even if it is simply what made them stand out to you in the first place. The most successful first lines forge a connection rather than go in for the kill.

▶ If someone chats you up, even if you look like Marilyn Monroe and average 50 hits a night, be nice about it – it took guts to come up to you. Lie if you have to and say you're sorry (lie), they seem brilliant (lie) and in other circumstances you would (lie), but you're seeing someone at the moment (lie lie lie), or you've just broken up with someone (lie), or you're just really not looking for someone in your life for a while (lie). Be funny if you can to lighten the mood. For example, say that your hamster died earlier in the day and you're too upset to contemplate romance (lie). Be polite while making your feelings clear. If someone turns you down, take the hint. Gather your pride, say 'that's a shame' and go back to your friends who delight in your company.

▶ Well mannered men and women may flirt with any number of people throughout one night, but only swap bodily fluids of any sort (including saliva) with one. Choose wisely though, for modern manners dictate that after that exchange, even flirting with another is poor practice.

▶ If the object of your affections hands you an email address for contact rather than a phone number, don't insist on digits. Distributing contact information is a personal choice.

▶ Do not deliberately hand out a wrong number. If you would prefer not to release it, take theirs instead. Under these circumstances there is no need to use it.

▶ Observe this crucial difference, ladies and gentlefolk: it is fair play not to call a number thrust onto you without your requesting it or as an act of defence because you did not want to give your own, but foul play to ask, unprompted, for a *contact detail and then not use it. If in a moment of drunken foolery you ignore this rule, your etiquette halo will only sit straight again by sending a short note briefly saying that you had a great time but you are just not dating at the moment.*

Dating

FIRST DATES

Whoever asks organizes. If you are the organizer, offer to pay and refuse twice if the other party mentions splitting the bill or paying. If the other party asks a third time with some force, or mentions at any point that it would make them more comfortable, let them split the bill. The organizer should never let their guest pay in full. Ideally, the organizer should pay when their guest leaves the table temporarily, thus avoiding the situation in its entirety.

Insight

Arrange first meetings in public places so that your date does not feel ambushed or at risk.

By the rule above, in heterosexual relationships, more often than not men find themselves saddled with cheque-writing duty as they are still more likely to initiate the date. Unless it seems to make the woman squirm (judged by using the paragraph above), a man should insist with enthusiasm without reference to feminism that he pays, perhaps with a throwaway phrase such as, 'You can get the next one' if he intends to see the lady again.

Start the date by explaining that there is somewhere that you should be later on, even if in truth that place is bed with a cup of tea. Stay for at least an hour. If, after this hour, it has become evident that you have no desire to see this person again, leave reciting the reason mentioned at the start. If after that hour you wish to extend the date, fake taking a call outside that cancels the arrangement. Only exit via a back door or bathroom window if you feel threatened. Do have a friend call to check that all is well from the point of view of safety, but not with an 'emergency' requiring your immediate assistance (you may as well say, 'Not only are you boring and ugly but I also think that you are stupid').

Talk about general subjects, for example, work, home, the weather, the tube. Stay off high-risk subjects such as abortion, euthanasia and exes. Topics that could trigger an emotional reaction are not ones to discuss on a first date, so don't bring them up. Don't enquire as to the date of their last STD test (unless you plan to have sex with them that evening). Don't ask how much they earn per year. Try, instead, light, friendly topics. First dates are about checking out the sparkling lights on the surface, not the currents underneath.

Although, as demonstrated in several areas of this book, good manners can force you to be downright stingy with the truth, do not say, 'I'll be in touch' if this is an outright lie. If in the panic to get away you suffer a bout of verbal platitude diarrhoea and a phrase such as this slips uncontrollably from your lips, email or text the next day with an excuse of some sort that leaves you incapable of dating for the moment (such as, 'I like you but I'm just not ready to be dating someone seriously' or, more honestly, 'You're a great person but I think maybe the chemistry isn't right').

Insight

Avoid the cinema for a first date. Your mind may already be made up but your date may want some time to talk to you to see if you are compatible.

SECOND DATES

Second dates should follow the same pattern as first dates. Whoever asks and organizes should make an effort to pay. The chosen topics of conversation may be a little riskier, but still bear in mind that you are not (yet) each other's best friends.

If it seems as though a topic is provoking an emotional reaction, it is better to change the subject than delve deeper.

THIRD DATES

It doesn't matter who asked. If by this point one person has already paid twice, it is the duty of the other person at this point to stump up the cash. In heterosexual relationships, this is likely to be a case of the man offering and the woman insisting. If, however, it is one all, either the organizer of the date pays or the bill is split. Conversational topics may dig a little deeper, but don't push someone into talking to you about something which clearly makes them uncomfortable.

FOURTH DATES AND BEYOND

Both parties should find some way of paying their own way, lest they become a financial burden. Just because a person thinks you are better than champagne on a sunny afternoon doesn't mean that their salary magically doubled upon your first kiss.

There is no 'correct' time to have sex with someone. Implying that someone has chosen the wrong time by actions or words is rude in the extreme. If you fall into bed with a partner on the first date, before branding a partner 'loose' or 'a slut', remember that it takes two to tango.

Wait to be asked to leave items in a partner's home. After six months, if this has not happened naturally, tell your partner that you need to leave a small bag of things at their house, rather than 'accidentally' leaving pieces behind. If you are sleeping with someone regularly, allow them to keep some things at your house. Accept the invasion of space with good grace, and apologize for not having suggested it yourself. Keep any discussion of exes to a minimum throughout the course of your relationship.

Some consider Valentine's Day to be heart-shaped commercial tripe. If you object to it on these grounds by all means do not ignore your principles, but neither should you ignore the day. Make your partner a card, run them a bath and make them supper.

Try to keep the number of times you stay at each other's houses even. It is always nicer to wake in your own bed, so share the privilege, even if one of you lives in a less convenient place.

SAFETY FIRST

Condoms should be bought by both partners. Everyone should have a discreet but convenient stash. The onus is mostly on the owner of the house to provide condoms, but it is best not to rely on this if you are gearing up for a big night in bed. Should they be required, the cost of morning after pills should also be shared.

With heterosexual couples, it is polite to ask ladies whether any form of birth control is already in place and whether they would still like you to use a condom. Never assume that a man is wearing his wellies or a lady is as pilled up as a hippy at Glastonbury.

It is reasonable (and safe) to ask a partner to have an STD test before you have sex with them. It is also reasonable to ask your partner to continue using a barrier method of protection. Rather than questioning where the dirty scoundrel may have been, claim it as a policy of yours. Never whine or complain in response to either of these requests.

A special note should be given to intrauterine devices (the coil) as a method of birth control. The coil, once in place, increases the chance of a woman catching a sexually transmitted infection and once the infection is present, it can cause infertility even more rapidly than in other women. Cheating on a female partner while she is using the coil and sleeping with her again without having a full STD test, is etiquettely and ethically wrong, devoid of morals or care. If you do this you deserve to be plagued with genital herpes for the rest of your sorry life.

Lying about pregnancy scares, the presence of STDs, STD tests or birth control being in place is poor form. Warn partners of any contagious diseases or infections you may be carrying before sexual activity. It is wise to do this before the bedroom is entered. It is also only fair to let your partner know if there is any other significant person in your life.

Meeting family and friends

Insight

Do make the effort to introduce your partner to your friends. Even if the worlds seem difficult to mix, it shows pride in both your friends and your new partner.

Ask your partner about their parents and siblings before you meet them, with particular emphasis on which topics will provoke a keen reaction from them and which ones will cause disgust and horror. If meeting the parents at their home, as much as your partner may insist that there is no need for a present, find out what the parents enjoy and take it upon yourself to bring a nice bottle of whiskey, wine, flowers or chocolates, or anything really that indicates some effort.

Parents – remember the name of the partner you are being introduced to. Forgetting it implies that your offspring has not deemed their partner important enough to talk to you about. Getting it wrong by, as is often the case, using the name of your offspring's ex or a friend of theirs, holds the implication that you wish that this new partner was in fact that person. Do not joke about babies or marriage, but do act as though you are embracing the new partner into the family, even if secretly you think they would never fit in.

Parents can follow the 'best friends criticizing a new partner' rules on page 186–187. If you are the partner, don't criticize your 'in-laws' even if your partner does.

The first time your new partner meets your parents, stay close. You may love both parties but they might not immediately become firm friends. Tease your partner as you would normally but remember that the partner is trying to make a good impression and that impression is likely be a reflection of how you act around them. Engage your partner and parents in conversation as a group. Remember that if you are sulky, your parents will undoubtedly see it as a result of the new partner's presence rather than the result of a hard week at work/the car not starting/Liverpool not winning the Champions League. Similarly, don't gang up against your partner in front of their close friends or relatives unless in total jest.

When meeting the parents for the first time, be particularly mindful of wearing something appropriate for the occasion and err on the side of conservative dressing, staying away from any outfit which may expose a thrilling amount of flesh. Don't drink too much alcohol during the meeting and always write a thank-you note if you have visited your 'in-laws' house.

If you are staying the night in separate rooms, any bed hopping must be done by the person to whom the parents belong.

Breaking up

WHEN YOU ARE THE DUMPER

After a first date, if you have no desire to remain friends, simply stop contact. If the other person tries to contact you, send a text to clarify the situation. At any time before the fourth date, a break-up email or text is okay. After a fourth date, a call at the very least is necessary. If either of you is referring to the other as a boyfriend/girlfriend/partner, a meeting is preferable, but a phone call may suffice if the relationship has been both casual and short-lived. If you are living together or married, you should speak face to face.

For those dumping their partners by letter, email or text, it is best to blame a lack of chemistry rather than any fault of yours or theirs. It is nice to mention that you find them physically attractive and great fun to be around (lie about this if necessary) but say that you simply do not feel a spark. Spell check it. Read it over at least twice to ensure that you have said all that is necessary to mark the end of the situation without including anything hurtful. Do not send a break-up email to a work address or a text during your soon-to-be-ex's working hours. Do not force them into suffering the indignity of having to hold back tears for the rest of their day at work.

Plan face-to-face or phone break-ups meticulously. Think of a suitable time and place and an outline of what you are going to say, or not say. It is inadvisable to warn your soon-to-be-ex that you 'need to have a chat', or some version of this phrase, unless you are prepared to break up then and there. There is never a good time to have a conversation which will inevitably hurt someone you care about, but some times are worse than others. For example, a Monday morning is not a good time as the injured party will likely then have to endure a tear-filled day at work and wait hours until a little alcoholic light relief can be sought. Any day of personal mourning is also a bad time.

Consider where to start the break-up. Do not choose their favourite bar or restaurant. It should not be done at either your home or theirs: breaking up at your home is lazy; breaking up at their home bequeaths to them a host of upsetting memories associated with a place which, for most, is one of peace and rest. Choose somewhere reasonably quiet but not romantic. Make the venue within easy access to their house, so that they can head home after the deed is done easily and with minimal embarrassment should they start crying on the bus.

Do not break up with your partner immediately after sex. If you do choose to break up with a partner while they are at your house late at night, perhaps even already in bed, you must offer to call a cab and pay for it to get them home or walk them back if the distance is easy. Failing either of these options, for example, if the situation makes this awkward (there are no cabs available and your now-ex lives 50 km away), you must offer to sleep on the floor or couch and relinquish your bed for the use of your ex.

Cowards – it is beyond reproach to make someone's life miserable for months or years in the hope that the other party will break up with you. Also, do inform the other person that you are breaking up, don't just stop returning calls.

Think about what you are going to say before you open your mouth. Clichés have evolved as the result of a widespread similarity of feeling, but the use of them reeks of a lack of thought or care. If a cliché does slip out, make sure to use only the one, acknowledge its use and use it only if you can justify it. Preferably use the justification without the cliché. Note: unless the other party has greatly wronged you, it is always you, never them.

There is limited need to be honest. Is it better to be lied to than hurt unnecessarily. Decide beforehand whether you want this to be a discussion about what needs to be changed in order for you to stay together or an announcement of the end. If the former, be as honest as possible. If the latter, give enough information to clarify the situation and no more.

Do not suggest ways that the other person could have made your time together better and do not give advice for future relationships. Should they want it, they will ask. Do not suggest break-up sex, or that you continue to sleep together for a while. One of you will be hoping that your relationship will regain a romantic status and it is likely not to be you. Do tell your ex that all your friends think that you are crazy for letting them go, even if said friends are actually dancing for joy and helped you compose your break-up strategy.

If it was serious, offer to set a date to see each other again. Call the person a few days later to check that they are okay. If they don't answer, try again the day after. If they still don't answer, respect that they don't want to see you again and stop calling. It was the chance you took in breaking up with them. Leave an answer phone message explaining that you would like to stay in touch but do not want to make a nuisance of yourself so you are leaving it up to them. Emphasize the difference between a lack of chemistry and a lack of friendship and respect.

If requested by your ex, have a post-break-up long conversation about what went wrong. That is your duty. After that, these conversations are a choice, not an obligation. Lie low for a week after the break-up. You should always say that it was a difficult decision, and you need to give the impression that you weren't lying. If you don't lie low, Murphy's law says that one of your ex's friends will see you partying hard singing 'I'm too sexy' the evening of your break-up and report the sorry news.

It is the job of the dumpee to decide how much they want to know about your new life. Do not force the information upon them. Do not bring new partners to places where you expect to see your ex for the next six months, or until you hear news that your ex is seeing someone else. If, at a later date, you overhear your ex gleefully saying that it was mutual, or that they dumped you, do not wade in to correct them. They are allowed this small white lie.

ETIQUETTE FOR BOTH HALVES OF THE BROKEN COUPLE

▶ *Don't tell all their friends or your own the horrible things your ex-partner once said about them.*
▶ *No matter how viciously they have wronged you, do not retaliate immediately by trying to get them fired, sleeping with their best friend or telling them that you have contracted an STD from them. Wait for a month. If you still want to retaliate, think through the consequences before taking action.*
▶ *Don't call, text or email late at night or when drunk.*
▶ *Don't hit on your ex's friends unless you suspect it may be true love. Even then, it is a mark of respect for your ex, even if you have no plans on staying in touch, to wait for months if not*

years, before making your feelings known. If you are still in touch with the ex, make your feelings officially known to the ex before your new love.

▶ *Let the dumpee set the date for the return of possessions. If this has not been done after two months, call to suggest the swap at a time of their convenience.*

▶ *Never bring new partners to venues that were special for you and another.*

▶ *If the break-up has come about as a result of a serious grievance, such as a repeatedly unfaithful partner or domestic violence, ignore all of the above. Just leave. There is no explanation necessary.*

FOR THE BROKEN-HEARTED

You may weep and wail once in front of your ex-partner. After that, refuse contact until you can pull it together. It is not productive to do anything else and only serves to make the other person feel bad. If you should meet your ex's new love interest, do not flirt with your ex in an attempt to assert control over the situation. This is an unprovoked attack on the emotions of the new partner. You should set the date for the return of possessions – make it within a fortnight of the break-up. If you want to save face, don't tell all your mutual friends that you made the decision, say it was mutual.

Combining partners and friends

Neither the new partner nor the friends should pass negative judgement immediately on each other. You owe it to your friends or partner to make an effort with the people they love. If you can't say anything nice, keep silent.

After three meetings, if you are a close friend and feel that your friend's new partner is unsuitable, or if you are the new partner and are unsure of the actions of one of your partner's friends, it is polite to tell. It would be better phrased, however, as a way of getting to know the person as there may be a reason for their ludicrous behaviour.

A close friend may criticize all manner of faults in the new boyfriend as long as they do it only once and start with a sentiment such as, 'but if these things don't bother you then of course it is fine, I'm just looking out for you' and finish with a similar statement. If your friend still wants to carry on seeing their new partner, that's their prerogative. Tell your friend that you are sure their new partner will grow on you with time and familiarity and consider whether any of the new partner's faults can be put down to nerves.

As the new partner, it is best to exercise an even greater degree of caution before criticizing the friends. Those friends were around for a while before you met your partner and will likely be around long after you leave. There may be reasons for odd behaviour from friends, such as old habits that are fine by your partner.

Friends should try to be nice to, but not flirt with, a friend's partner. Neither should they deliberately wear suggestive clothing in order to attract admiring glances from a friend's partner. Hot pants and a bra are not appropriate attire for watching Sunday morning television if your flatmate brought someone back on Saturday night. The only exception would be if the couple were gay and you were of the opposite sex – but even then it may cause a few blushes.

With a new partner, it is often easy in the first heady days of love to talk non-stop about the new person in your life. This is not fair on your single friends. They love you and are pleased that you are happy, but do not need to know that you love the way your partner eats his cereal or puts on her socks. Most friends will find this chatter sick-making but understandable for the first month. After this period of grace, such talk becomes loathsome and is likely to lose you friends.

When you become attached to a significant other, the time available to spend with your friends shrinks. Manage your time to make sure you include your friends and partner. Make arrangements to see your friends and do not break them in favour of seeing your partner. Similarly, if you have made an arrangement with your partner, do not break it to hear the latest gossip about who slept with who at the school reunion.

One of the golden rules about friends is that their secrets are to be told to nobody. This includes your partner.

During a break-up friends are advised to make themselves available but to think carefully about pitching in to bad-mouth the ex. Friends may agree with the list of awful things about your ex spilling forth from your lips, particularly if they can find humorous examples of such grievances. However, until the break-up is cemented, the phrase, 'Well I never liked him anyway', complete with an additional list of character assassinations, is best avoided. If a friend does get carried away in the moment and you do reunite with your estranged partner, remember that what was said was a defence of you rather than an attack on your other half.

For the purpose of a relationship, acquaintances should wait six months before moving in on a friend's ex. Fully fledged friends should wait 18 months. Best friends, ideally never. In all circumstances, permission should be sought from your friend before the first date and the granting of that permission should not be assumed. If the friend does not bless you to dally with their ex as you see fit, consider it a direct choice between your friend and your budding relationship.

As a general rule, with places, possessions and friends, each part of a severed couple leaves with that with which they arrived. If, however, a close friendship has developed over the years, friends may stay in touch with a friend's ex. Flaunting this, however, by inviting both halves of a split couple to the same parties or talking incessantly about them, is bad manners, particularly if the couple in question no longer speak.

Friends do not have one night stands or become f**k buddies with a friend's ex. The presence of a bottle of vodka does not constitute an exception.

Argument etiquette

Don't hit below the belt. Don't bring in the opinions of others to hit below the belt. This is between the two of you, and not a point-scoring debate. Once an argument is settled, try not to return to it later.

Insight

If you have a grievance, write it down. Leave the matter for 24 hours and re-read what you have written. If you are still angry, give careful consideration to how to broach the topic. Always attempt to talk about the problem rather than immediately writing a letter or email, only use the latter methods if talking makes it difficult for you to express exactly what you mean out loud.

10 THINGS TO REMEMBER

1 *Both men and women can make the first move.*

2 *If turning someone down, do it politely and with as little hurt to their feelings as possible.*

3 *If you ask for someone's number, use it.*

4 *Whoever asks for a date organizes it and offers to pay.*

5 *Practise safe sex and feel free to ask questions to ascertain what protection is in place.*

6 *Make an effort with family and friends.*

7 *If a break-up is pre-meditated, think carefully about how to do it to cause the least hurt, including where you meet, when and what you say.*

8 *If you are the dumper, lie low after a break-up and try to avoid making the situation worse by being seen with a new partner in the near future.*

9 *Never lie about pregnancy control or scares, STD tests or the presence of STDs.*

10 *Even if one half of the couple earns more than the other, the poorer half should make sure that the richer half does not always foot the bill.*

14

Surviving special occasions

In this chapter you will learn how to:
- *treat new parents*
- *attend a wedding*
- *support mourners*
- *help celebrate a special day.*

Chunky volumes have been written on the etiquette of weddings, stag nights and showers in detail too great to try to cover here. In this modern day if it is your special day – whether that be your wedding or your time as chief mourner – chances are whatever you choose will be met with approval, whether that be a big white wedding and engraved invitations or screaming 'I do' as you bungee jump the Grand Canyon. Provided you are considerate of the feelings of others and make an effort to treat all close family members similarly, few will object, or indeed have the right to object, to whatever you choose. This, instead, is a guide for the event-goer, who is likely to offend time and time again if they are unaware of the correct etiquette.

Births

TRADITIONAL BIRTHS

Only the father/partner or one or two close friends should be present for the actual birthing experience, although very close friends and family may visit at the hospital shortly after the birth, bringing cards or gifts to convey their congratulations.

When the mother and child return home, bear in mind that their house may become a nest of chaos and sleep deprivation. Offer to help where possible with the cleaning of the house, running errands or other chores. Do not go to the house without giving warning, even if you are in the habit of doing so. Consider sending texts rather than telephoning after 5 p.m. or during times that you know the baby is scheduled to sleep. If you invite the parents of a newborn (less than six months old) to lunch or supper, understand if they decline owing to tiredness or are unwilling to leave the child with a carer. If they do attend, do not expect the favour returned soon.

Within a week of a healthy birth, you should receive an email or snail mail announcement of the child's arrival, giving details of weight, length and time of birth and perhaps a photo. Reply with words of congratulation and send a gift if there was no baby shower.

Insight

As an expectant mother's due date approaches, don't continually call to ask if the baby has turned up yet. Chances are that the new mum would have already somehow let the world know of the arrival and if there have been any complications in birth, the parents will not want an inundation of calls awaiting happy news.

DIFFICULT BIRTHS

If the baby is stillborn, do not expect the parents to announce the birth. If the child is born with a disability, it is up to the parents whether they want to announce the birth, depending on the severity of the disability and, if so, whether they want to announce the disability with it – do not pressure the parents into doing either of these.

If the child is born with a disability, the parents may have to spend much time at the hospital. If this is the case, offer help where possible, such as keeping their house in order in their absence and running errands. If the child is stillborn, treat the parents as you would those who had lost an older child or other close family member (see below). Under no circumstances make any suggestion that the parents' loss is any less than the loss of a fully grown child.

ADOPTION

When adopting a newborn, family and friends should fuss around and give the same help as they would if the baby was genetically related. New mothers of adopted children will still need help, so provide it when you can. When the adoption is of an older child, ask the parents what can be done to help the family adjust and the adoptee to settle in.

TERMINATIONS, MISCARRIAGES AND GIVING BABIES UP FOR ADOPTION

After a termination, a miscarriage or the giving of a baby for adoption, keep quiet on the subject and do all that you can to help the woman return to a 'normal' life as soon as possible. Don't bring up the topic of conversation yourself; wait for it to be raised by the person in question. If the subject does arise, be a good listener. If the miscarriage was late in the pregnancy, the parents may feel grief comparable to the death of a stillborn. Treat them with the respect that mourners deserve (see below). If the pregnancy was terminated or the baby given up for adoption, don't be judgemental. Don't project your own beliefs onto the person in question.

Deaths

In the event of a death, it is often difficult to know the best thing to do or what to say. People deal with grief differently, but in times of sadness it is often sufficient just to let the mourner know that you are there for them. Even if you only know the mourner rather than the mourned, do at least send a card and don't expect a reply. In the card, write a short note expressing friendship, love and care for the mourner, and the mourned (if you knew them). If you have strong religious views which might help, you may explain them. Call if you are a friend rather than an acquaintance, and offer to help in any way you can in liaising with funeral directors, etc. Visit if possible and send flowers if family and close friends have not specifically requested otherwise. Never congratulate a person on the receipt of inheritance – what was gained is the result of a loss that is likely to have far outweighed any monetary benefit.

As a close friend of a mourner, even if you did not know the person who died, you should attend the funeral as a show of support, unless your mourning friend insists otherwise for a specific reason that makes it more convenient for them.

Insight

At a funeral, wear what you are told to by the organizers, even if this does not fit with the traditional black conservative outfit you consider appropriate. Close family may have some unusual ideas for an appropriate send off, but these should all be respected. Don't harass the bereaved with minor questions regarding the funeral – instead ask a close friend of the bereaved.

Remember that many initial offerings of support can fade away after the first month, but the grief does not. Keep re-offering your support for at least the first year after a death, if in no other way than your frequent presence in the mourner's life. Try to remember the anniversary of the death as well as any other anniversaries involving the deceased. Provide extra support on these days, for example, birthdays or wedding anniversaries. Also remember that days which would normally involve the deceased (for example, Christmas or the mourner's birthday) may be particularly difficult and show extra support for the first few years after the death.

Showers

Bridal and baby showers are commonly given up to three months before the wedding or the birth of the child. In Britain, it is not usual to register at a shop for shower presents, but it is worth checking with the host (usually a close friend or sibling) to find out whether a registry does exist and if not whether the bride has specifically asked for any items in particular. At bridal showers, gifts are given specifically for the bride rather than the couple. At baby showers, appropriate presents are given first and foremost for the baby, but also for the new mother.

Hen and stag nights

However raucous the event, all hen and stag nights should have one theme in common: 'Get them to the church on time'. On a stag or hen night, the stag or hen can do pretty much whatever they please to have a good time, provided that they do nothing to jeopardize the happiness of the upcoming marriage and that they are left able to arrive at the wedding on time and in a reasonable condition. In particular, it is worth noting that having sex with anyone other than your fiancé(e) on any night is considered cheating, so don't pressure the hen or stag into it. It is often better to have the hen or stag night/weekend/week at least a month before the wedding so that the other half of the couple is not left struggling with the last-minute arrangements for the big day.

Weddings

Respond promptly to a wedding invitation. The guest list may be confined to a small number due to venue size and your non-attendance could mean that the couple may be able to invite another of their friends.

When attending a marriage, it is bad form to wait until the 'Are there any objections to this marriage' part of the ceremony to object. If you do have any objection, state it before the bride gets dressed for her big day, calmly and with good reason in quiet surroundings.

Never attend a wedding if you have had or are having an affair with either the bride or groom or plan to do so. Also, never flirt with the bride or groom on their big day.

Do not bring presents to the reception or ceremony as they are likely to be forgotten in the commotion. Deliver them before the big day to the couple's residence. If the couple has registered at a particular store, make an effort to purchase something from the list. If the couple has not registered, make sure to buy a gift for the couple rather than just for whichever member of the couple you are closer to. Weddings are costly – if you are invited, be generous with your gift, even if you cannot attend the wedding.

In the run up to a wedding, if you are part of the wedding party, (e.g. a bridesmaid or usher), expect to be laden with numerous duties. Carry them out with good humour. Also, whatever the outfit chosen for you, it is your duty to wear it without a whisper of a complaint.

Follow directions on the invitation regarding the dress code. If the invitation does not specify a dress code, consider it either day or evening formal, depending on the time of day of the event. If there is no mention of confetti being forbidden on the invitation, assume that it is welcome.

Insight

Take note of which parts of the wedding day you are invited to. Some couples only have close family at the church and/or wedding breakfast, but everyone to celebrate in the evening.

SECOND MARRIAGES

The ceremony is likely to be small for a second marriage, so do not to be offended if you are not invited. However, if you are a guest at a second marriage, any mention of the previous husband or wife (even in jest) is considered poor form.

Religious ceremonies

Religious ceremonies such as christenings, confirmations and bar mitzvahs should be attended where possible without reservation by those of other faiths who are invited. Attending will not be considered a relinquishing of your own faith – you are not required to join in the chantings of a different faith or any of the ceremonial parts, but your presence is considered supportive of the person there. If you feel uncomfortable attending, instead make sure to send a card and present.

Graduations

The seats for graduation ceremonies are normally limited so unless you are a parent or sibling, don't expect to be invited, or indeed receive an explanation as to why you were not invited.

Do send a congratulations card to the graduand and, if you want to, a present. Make it a priority to attend a graduation party if one is thrown for the graduand. Appropriate presents are those which can act as a keepsake, for example books or CDs.

Hospital visits

If a friend or relative must spend more than 24 hours in hospital, particularly for surgery, check that they have someone accompanying them. If not, where possible rearrange your schedule so that you can volunteer yourself. If the person must spend more than 48 hours in hospital, visit bringing a thoughtful gift, such as flowers or something to keep the patient amused such as magazines or puzzle books.

Birthdays

Birthday parties are more important than normal nights out, so if a birthday party is organized, reschedule other friends where possible in order to attend. Send presents and cards in time for the birthday, not the party. Always call, text or email with good wishes for the next year on the actual day.

Insight

Giving birthday presents to friends somehow seems childish after teenage years, but continue doing so. Even the smallest most inexpensive present will be received with great appreciation if thought and effort is attached to the gift.

10 THINGS TO REMEMBER

1 *Understand that parents of newborns may be sleep deprived and may cancel at the last minute.*

2 *Never raise the topic of terminations, adoptions or stillbirths. Let the parents choose whether to talk about it or not.*

3 *Re-offer support and help in coping time and time again for the first year after the close relative of someone dies.*

4 *Give gifts to the bride at bridal showers and gifts to the baby and mother at baby showers.*

5 *Hen and stag nights should be as raucous as the bride or groom desires, but don't force either into activities that may threaten the relationship in the future.*

6 *Respond promptly to wedding invitations and follow to the letter any instructions therein.*

7 *Understand when seating is limited at certain events such as graduations and you have not been invited.*

8 *Even if a party has been organized for a different day than the achievement, remember to call or text to send good wishes on the actual day.*

9 *Be respectful of others' choices of religious ceremonies to celebrate and where possible attend, even if it is not the most fun experience.*

10 *Prioritize special occasions in the lives of friends and family over regular days or nights out.*

15

....

Disabilities

In this chapter you will learn how to:
- *refer to disabled people and disabilities*
- *treat disabled people*
- *help people with disabilities.*

People with disabilities tend to make others nervous, mostly because those without the disability find it hard to empathize and so do not instinctively know how the person with the disability would like to be treated. The most important thing to remember, though, is that no matter what the disability, the person in front of you is human, capable of communication in some sense and deserves the same respect as someone without the disability.
Do this and you can barely go wrong.

Basics

Try to do the following:

- ▶ *Use the same action of greeting (kissing or shaking a hand) that you would with anyone else. Hold out a hand to shake when you meet a person with a disability, even if they have limited use of their arms. The action of personal contact shows acceptance.*
- ▶ *Make eye contact. Talk to the person rather than the wheelchair or the carer or guide dog if they are with one.*

Similarly, if the person is deaf, talk face to face and make eye contact with the deaf person rather than their sign language interpreter.

▶ *Do not stare at areas of wasted muscle mass or missing limbs; it is as inappropriate as staring at a women's breasts or a man's crotch as you speak to them.*

▶ *Talk normally. Do not shout at those who are lip reading or speak especially slowly for those who are blind. There is no need to apologize for phrases such as 'see you later' if said to a blind person.*

▶ *If someone has difficulty understanding you, be patient and be prepared to explain something more than once in a variety of ways.*

▶ *Do not use behaviour more appropriate for dealing with children, for example, literally or figuratively patting a wheelchair user on the head.*

▶ *Guide dogs for people with disabilities are working dogs, not cute pets. Distracting them by feeding or patting them puts their owners in danger. Similar treatment should be exercised with puppies in training for such a job.*

▶ *Don't ask personal questions about a person's disability, such as 'Were you born blind?' or 'So how do you have sex?' If they want to talk about it, they will volunteer the information or topic of conversation over time. If they don't want to, they won't.*

▶ *If you are unsure what to do or how a particular situation will affect a person with a disability, always ask the person with the disability the correct action to take to help them. Everyone is different but each person is in the prime position to know how best they can be aided. Offer assistance if you think it is needed, but wait for a positive reply to your suggestion before you continue. Do not make assumptions about a disabled person's abilities. They have developed methods of overcoming many everyday problems.*

▶ *If you have children, they might stare. Talk to the child about people with disabilities to help them understand why people use wheelchairs or communicate differently. This will help to prevent fearful and negative attitudes towards people with disabilities.*

Wheelchair users

If a conversation is more than a passing 'hello', stand back or try to find somewhere to sit so that you are both on the same eye level in order to reduce strain on the wheelchair user's neck.

The wheelchair is part of the wheelchair user's personal space. Don't rest items or any part of your body on their wheelchair, lean on it or touch it unless the wheelchair user indicates that this is okay. Never move an occupied wheelchair without permission from the user. Always ask first and wait for a response as upsetting their balance could be dangerous.

If a wheelchair user is visiting you in a building which you know well but they do not, make sure that they know how to access the building or meet them at the entrance to show them the way. If you are organizing a meeting at which you know a wheelchair user will be in attendance, choose a venue with disabled access.

Never slap a disabled person on the back or thigh even as a gesture of goodwill or jest as if they have spinal cord injuries, this could trigger muscle spasms. Always use a light touch.

The hearing impaired

Find out as soon as possible how the person will find it easiest to communicate with you, for example, if the person has a sign language interpreter or lip reads. Use a pen and paper to determine this if there is no other obvious method. If they lip read, make sure that your face is clearly visible (not obstructed by your hands or headwear), that you are facing the person and that you speak slowly but naturally (exaggerated lip movements make lip reading difficult). Don't smoke or eat while someone is trying to read your lips.

If the person does lip read but they cannot understand something you have said, rephrase the comment or question as different lip movements may be easier to decipher. Be aware that it is a skill which requires intense concentration and thus may be tiring. If an interpreter is present, make eye contact with the hearing-impaired person, not the interpreter. There is no need to shout unless you are naturally showing emotion.

To attract the person's attention, do so with a light touch on their shoulder or wave. If possible, position yourself such that neither of these come as a complete surprise to the person you approach.

The visually impaired

When meeting someone with a visual impairment, introduce yourself as you would on the telephone. Also introduce anyone else who is present with you, giving a brief description of their position with respect to the person with the visual impairment. Each of these people should then say hello in order that the visually impaired person can get a handle on identifying the voices. When you decide to move away, tell the person with the visual impairment what you are doing and say goodbye or you could leave them talking to air.

Offer a handshake or a kiss but say something such as, 'Let's shake hands' or 'I must give you a kiss hello' to indicate your intention.

Rather than pushing or pulling a blind person in order to guide them, ask if they would like to take hold of your arm. When guiding them, give descriptive warnings of any obstacles such as steps or potholes.

When meeting a visually impaired person outside their home, offer to meet them at a point with which they are familiar and travel the rest of the journey together to anywhere new.

When offering a seat, speak the person through the process, giving the direction of the chair from the person or placing the person's hand on it. When giving directions, make them as precise as possible and try to give a sense of distance rather than relying only on landmarks. For example, instead of 'At the opticians, turn left and go up the stairs,' say, 'At the opticians, about 200 metres down the street, turn left up the stairs – there are only two or three'.

Insight

Be mindful that in restaurants or other situations where decisions need to be made from visual information, you will need to provide the aural equivalent by reading a menu or describing a situation. Do so slowly in order to give the person a chance to absorb the information they will need to make their choice.

Those with speech impairments

When you are talking to someone with a speech impairment, concentrate on what is being said, be patient and never finish their sentences for them. If you don't understand, don't pretend you do. To aid the process, consider repeating what was understood and have the person with the speech impairment finish the rest. If you are in a noisy area, move to somewhere quieter. Ask questions that require short answers if you sense that speaking is making the person uncomfortable.

Do not make assumptions about the person's hearing. Some people with speech impairments can hear perfectly well, others cannot. Wait for the disabled person to indicate that they have a hearing impairment before asking whether the person can lip read or requires an interpreter.

Other disabilities

Other disabilities are varied and often it is difficult to ascertain what exactly needs to be done to make the person comfortable. It may also be difficult to ask those with mental disabilities for an explanation. Some may not be aware of social boundaries such as personal space, others may not like physical contact and some may appear aloof. Correct personal space intrusions and ask before touching, even shaking hands. Do not take offence or be embarrassed by whatever happens out of the 'norm' as a result of the disability.

Be clear in your communication. If in doubt, use words literally and simply. Never make the mistake of confusing intellect with communication difficulties.

Insight

Never be afraid of asking a disabled person what can be done to help them. It is better to ask and be thought to be fussing that not ask and be thought callous and uncaring

Mind your language

When referring to disabled people, the correct term is 'disabled people' or 'a person with a disability'. 'The disabled', 'handicapped', 'invalid' and 'cripple' may all be offensive to a disabled person.

Insight

If you hear someone else use a term which may cause offence to a disabled person, change the topic and if you are friends, explain in private as soon as possible that the terminology may cause offence.

Phrases to watch out for include:

Risky	Safer
Confined to a wheelchair	Wheelchair user ('confined' implies restriction rather than freedom)
Intellectual impairment Mental handicap	Learning difficulties
The deaf	Deaf people or hearing impaired
The blind	Blind people or visually impaired
Disabled toilets	Accessible toilets
Care worker	Personal assistant
The disabled Invalid Handicapped Cripple	Disabled people or a person with a disability
Suffers from Struggling against	'Living with' or 'has'
For wheelchairs	For wheelchair users

Insight

Don't continually use your disabled friend as spokesperson for disabled people, or indeed a spokesperson for their particular disability. For the most part, they are likely to want to be treated as though their disability is not glaringly obvious to a group.

10 THINGS TO REMEMBER

1 *Treat people with disabilities as normally as possible.*

2 *Make eye contact and do not stare at missing limbs or areas of wasted muscle.*

3 *Consider a wheelchair as an extension of the person using it and give it its own personal space.*

4 *Do not distract guide dogs by feeding them or playing with them without checking with their owner first.*

5 *Find out at the start of a conversation how someone with impaired hearing finds it easiest to communicate.*

6 *When talking to someone with a speech impairment, concentrate on what is being said, be patient and do not finish sentences.*

7 *Never confuse poor intellect with communication difficulties.*

8 *Mind your language. Some terms regarding disabilities are very offensive.*

9 *Don't ask questions about a person's disability unless encouraged to do so.*

10 *When meeting a sight-impaired person outside their home, make it somewhere they know or can get to easily so that you can guide them from there.*

16

The heterosexual's guide to homosexuality

In this chapter you will learn how to:
- *refer to homosexuals*
- *respond to a coming-out*
- *recognize difficult situations, occasions, or uncomfortable topics of conversation for homosexuals or bisexuals*
- *act at gay weddings and divorces.*

Basics

Despite homosexual or transgendered people using all sorts of words to describe themselves, the following words should not be used by heterosexual people: queer, fag, dyke, butch, femme, camp, homo, hom, trannie, queen. Neither can you use phrases such as 'batting for the other team' or any other euphemism.

You must stick strongly to the following: gay (for both men and women), lesbian, transgendered, transexual or homosexual ('homosexual' is less common than the others but accurate – eyebrows may be raised at the use of the technical term but no offence will be taken). Follow the lead of a homosexual couple as to how they refer to each other – 'partner', 'spouse', 'boyfriend', 'girlfriend' or 'lover'. All of these have their own positive and negative connotations, so try to wait to see which the couple prefers. Despite the strictly business feeling, 'partner' is the safest bet if you are unsure.

Coming out

HOMOSEXUALITY

When a gay person comes out to you, your reaction to the situation can lose or keep you a friend, so it's important to get it right. Here are a few simple suggestions for coping with the announcement with good grace:

▶ *Don't out a person to himself or herself. Even if they mince like spaghetti bolognese and are camper than a boy scout, if they haven't decided on their sexual preference or decided to go public with it, you shouldn't either. Don't try to force a coming-out, particularly if the job of your potentially homosexual friend makes such a coming-out particularly awkward (for example, the military services, clergy members, teachers).*

▶ *Don't question it. The words 'are you sure?' should not cross your lips. Of course they're sure.*

▶ *Don't immediately ask difficult questions, such as those about religion, their prospects for having children or whether they are out to their family.*

▶ *Feign surprise, even if their homosexuality seems obvious. Try to keep your emotions under control, not showing a total lack of surprise or excessive shock. Don't underplay the announcement or make it seem like a shocking discovery.*

▶ *Don't arrogantly assume that the reason you are being told is because you are the object of their affections.*

▶ *Don't make a connection between homosexuality and gender confusion. These two are separate issues.*

▶ *Try to make sure that at some point after your friend has come out that you have some form of physical contact so that your friend knows that you don't think them repulsive.*

If you are used to hugging the friend, do so now. Never move away immediately after being told. Avoid all body language and verbal language of repulsion or shame.

▶ *Make an extra effort to maintain regular contact for the first few months after the coming-out so that your friend knows that you weren't feigning normality around them.*

▶ *If a close friend or a family member has told you that they are gay, it is because they want you to stay close. Even if you initially feel a little strange about it, don't reveal this. Support them and wait for the feeling to pass.*

▶ *If you are a sibling, as a result of your age you are likely to be more accepting of the announcement than your parents. Be supportive of your gay sibling in front of your parents. This is not an opportunity for you to steal the crown of favourite child. If there is a new partner, parents, siblings and close friends should express an interest in meeting him or her.*

▶ *If you are an ex, what you can ask will depend upon your relationship now with the person. If you are close enough to ask questions, ask out of curiosity, not anger. Don't ask if you caused 'it' – homosexuality is not a situational affliction or disease.*

▶ *If your partner comes out to you as gay, this is the end of your relationship. This is not an elaborate excuse for breaking up with you. It is the truth. Of course you will be upset, but try to take it without losing your temper – the person who has come out means you no harm and probably thinks much of you if they have bothered to tell you the real reason.*

BISEXUALITY

If someone comes out to you as bisexual, all of the above rules apply, but the two points below should also be noted.

▶ *Don't make comments inferring that the bisexual person just can't decide or is more promiscuous than a gay or straight person.*

▶ *If your partner tells you that they are bisexual, don't assume that this means that you must be breaking up. It was probably difficult to tell you so wait for them to explain what this means for your relationship before jumping to conclusions.*

Who can you tell?

Once a friend has confided in you that they are gay, you need to be careful about where you spread their news. The rules for this will depend on who the gay person in question is telling on their own.

Be cautious – it is better to look stupid than to spread (sometimes confidential) knowledge such as this. Think about the person's method of having come out to you – if it was done nervously and shyly by a close friend, it is probably a secret you should guard more closely than you do your own most intimate secrets; if it was done in passing by an acquaintance who is clearly telling all who will listen, less caution is required. However, always exercise particular caution around parents and employers. No matter how liberal the homosexual may be, don't make the mistake of assuming that they are out to these people. Always check with your friend first.

If the coming out was accidental, for example, walking in on a friend, apologize briefly but find your friend as soon as possible after the event to assure them that their secret is safe with you. Then don't bring the topic up again.

Don't talk about your friend's homosexuality loudly in public. They may not want to draw attention to their sexual preferences with unknown listeners milling about who may know their parents, employers, etc.

Unsuitable topics of conversation

Don't flaunt straight 'privileges'. Don't talk incessantly about your kids, wedding or large happy family gatherings if you know that the gay person you are speaking to has trouble with their family accepting their way of life. You shouldn't ask straight couples whether they plan to marry or have children, but this is even more important for gay couples as the complications and logistics can be even more difficult to overcome.

Don't discuss homosexual issues with your gay friends in public. It is not your gay friend's duty to be a spokesperson for their 'kind' and for them the conversation will seem more like a defence of their way of life than an even debate. If they want to speak about it then that's fine, but don't raise the topic yourself and if another straight person starts the conversation, you would do well to swiftly change it. Your gay friend is not a personal tour guide to the great world of homosexuality.

If a straight person makes homophobic comments, try to stop them before the gay person in their company does. It should be everyone's duty to correct a homophobe's ideas.

Straight weddings and births

Be aware that when you have a wedding, a hen night, a stag night or a christening, a gay person may feel resentful about attending, planning or helping as these events highlight that homosexuals have not yet been entirely accepted as equals. To some gay people, being asked to provide their presence and presents at one of these events is asking them to agree that this inequality is fair. Although gay marriage is now legal in some places around the world, cooing over the happy couple is done with gritted teeth by many parents; marriage in a church reminds gay people that 'God' does not bless their way of life; hen or stag nights often involve a stripper of the opposite sex which could put the homosexual attending in an uncomfortable situation; and christenings can remind gay people that even in a couple, only one partner at most will be able to supply DNA for the child.

Use some discretion when inviting homosexuals to these occasions. Of course some gay people may not find any of the above offensive and would not dream of missing a special day of yours. Do invite, but make it clear (without stating your take on the situation) that you will not be offended if they choose not to attend.

If your gay friend has a partner, invite them. It will help remind your friend of the reason they have made a more difficult lifestyle choice. At all turns, try not to force your gay friend into acting heterosexual for the day. Also, give some thought as to seating plans – don't be so foolish as to sit your gay friends next to known homophobes.

Insight

If you are the gay person deciding on whether to go to a wedding or the celebration of a birth, if you can do so without seeming resentful, do make the effort to go. It is a celebration which a couple want their friends to join, and whether that celebration is a birth, wedding, sporting achievement or promotion, they want your support.

Gay weddings

Give a couple having a gay wedding all the consideration and presents that you would a straight couple. Err on the side of formality and take care not to introduce a sense of irony to the day if the couple have not indicated that this is the expected form.

If a gay couple are married or living together, treat them exactly the same as you would treat a straight married couple, inviting them as a couple to events, for example.

Divorce

If your gay friends have had a gay marriage and divorce, give them the same consideration that you would a heterosexual married couple going through similarly hard times. Also bear in mind that 'divorce' consideration should be given to gay couples who have merely been living together without the ceremony of marriage, as many gay couples find the ceremony pointless without the blessing of parents or the Church, for example. If the couple have had children genetically born to one of the parents, also be aware of the added stress this may provide as one of them may now have no legal right to the child.

10 THINGS TO REMEMBER

1 *Mind your language. Some terms to describe gay people, lesbians, transgenders or transsexuals are offensive.*

2 *Let a person come out in their own time and don't question their choice when they do.*

3 *Make an extra effort to keep in touch shortly after a coming out to ensure that the person knows that their sexual orientation has not alienated you.*

4 *Never make comments that homosexuals and bisexuals are more promiscuous than straight people.*

5 *Be careful who you pass the news of a coming-out to.*

6 *Don't flaunt straight privileges such as marriage (in some countries) or having children. Understand that gay people may feel resentful about getting deeply involved in such 'straight' events.*

7 *Whether gay or straight, break-ups and divorce are traumatic experiences. Treat them as such.*

8 *Treat gay couples as straight couples. Invite both to events where partners are invited, for example.*

9 *Give a gay wedding all the considerations that would be afforded a straight marriage.*

10 *Do not use your gay friend as a spokesperson for their 'people' when talking in a group.*

17

Sporting etiquette

In this chapter you will learn how to:
- *play nicely with others*
- *use a gym*
- *use a changing room.*

General sporting etiquette

General points to bear in mind:

▶ *No one likes a gloating winner or a sore loser. No matter the outcome, shake your opponent's hand.*

▶ *Don't bet against your friends. If you are caught doing so, explain to them that it's only because you'll be so upset if they lose that you'll need something to cheer you up.*

▶ *Follow the rules of the game. Get a copy of the rule book to avoid arguments. If you know there are several versions of a rule, before you commence playing, determine which version you are going to follow. If possible appoint a referee for difficult calls.*

▶ *Play fair. Never grab the dangly bits.*

▶ *Never assume that you can teach yourself a notoriously dangerous sport or a sport in which incompetence could put the good health of yourself or others at risk. Take lessons if you need to and, until you are fully competent, stay out of the way of experts.*

▶ *If an area is normally used by a particular group and there is no formal or informal booking system, take the time to find out when the group uses the area. If you both arrive at the same time, regulars take priority.*

▶ *If an area is used for two different sports (for example, surfers and boogie boarders), stay well away from each other as the movements of a different sport are more unpredictable that those of your own sport.*

▶ *Don't rest in dangerous or inconvenient places. Get off the sporting ground.*

▶ *For sportsmen or women on their own, for example skiing or snowboarding, it is particularly important to offer your assistance if you see that someone is hurt or requires help.*

▶ *Arrive at the sporting area on time and ready to participate. Don't dress yourself in clothing or equipment in the sporting area – dress on the sidelines or in the changing rooms.*

▶ *Be mindful of the equipment of others, even if it is in your way. Make sure that your own equipment is not resting in an inconvenient place for others or being transported in a way which is unsafe.*

▶ *Never deliberately hurt someone else during a sporting endeavour, even in jest. However, if you accidentally hurt someone, apologize and wait to check that they are okay, giving them any assistance required.*

▶ *Never advance to a level that you know is outside your competency if that level may put you or others in danger.*

Insight

Sports are fun, but to keep them fun for everyone, play within your own ability range and be mindful of your shortcomings that may cause danger for others. Where possible warn others of a potential lack of control.

Gym etiquette

Going to the gym is a messy experience and can involve almost as much contact with other people's bodily fluids as, well, a far more intimate scenario. With varying amounts of experience, a likely invasion of personal space and hygiene not at its most fragrant, tempers sometimes flare over the slightest impoliteness. Counter-intuitive as it may seem that a place where grunting, sweating profusely and gurning is the norm, the rules of etiquette for a gym are as strict as at the opera or ballet (and for most, far more frequently needed). Try to adhere to the following:

▶ *Wipe down machines after use. If people want to swim, they will use the pool, not the leg press.*

▶ *If you must have your mobile in the gym, keep it on silent to avoid disturbing others. Do not have loud, long conversations into it while on a machine. This is not an exercise in multi-tasking – it is about fitness.*

▶ *Put weights away after use. People are not all built the same and it is safer for people to not have to move your weights.*

▶ *Share your equipment. When in between sets, offer the machine to a waiting bystander in your rests.*

▶ *You may end up dirty but you and your clothing should start clean.*

▶ *The drinking fountain is for the consumption of water, not a gum depositary. When there is a queue, do not fill large bottles.*

▶ *Don't drop or bang equipment. It's not good for the equipment and is distracting to those around you.*

▶ *Chat later. If you see an old friend, don't hog a machine while you talk about your marriage/kids/work, and don't stand by your friend's machine forcing them to hold a conversation as they struggle for breath. Instead, arrange to meet later.*

▶ *Often equipment has time limit recommendations attached and these should be adhered to in order to avoid monopolizing the machinery.*

▶ *Don't offer unsolicited advice. If someone is doing something potentially dangerous, tell a worker at the gym. They have the authority to approach the person and make the correction.*

▶ *Don't do lifts beyond your weight range.*

▶ *Don't walk in front of people using the mirror. Equally, don't stand a long distance away and expect the view to stay clear.*

- *Don't stare at or hit on people. Talk to them in reception if necessary. No one likes being perved on as they struggle to breathe with the effort of exertion.*
- *Wear clothing and supportive underwear suitable for working out. Items which ride up to expose more that you would like in a nightclub are not suitable. Stick to the house rules on the type of trainer sole allowed as some damage the floor. Expect people to look at you if you wear a skintight lycra G-string body suit ensemble, or anything along similar lines.*

Insight

Remember that for many, gym going is a deliberately solitary activity. Smile, but don't start a conversation unless it is clear that it is welcome and don't distract someone in the process of using machinery.

Changing room etiquette

Try to follow these guidelines:

- *Treat a changing room as a neater version of your own bathroom. Don't leave a mess behind and use a maximum of two towels.*
- *Use the changing cubicles if they are available. No one likes seeing your intimate wobbly bits if it can be helped.*
- *If you bump into a friend or work colleague when you are both choosing lockers, ask your friend whether they would prefer finding adjacent lockers or ones further apart. If the friend has already chosen a locker, unless they motion to a free locker near them, choose one further away, preferably out of the sight of your friend. If you use the same gym as your boss, make an excuse to choose a locker far away from them, even if that excuse is quite simply 'routine'.*
- *Don't stare. Strange body parts and towel usage will be on display in changing rooms. Ignore anything that seems out of the usual, as morbidly fascinating as it may be.*

- Use a towel to dry yourself. Don't wave it around triumphantly after using it or start a towel smack fight with your friends.
- Make any sort of romantic intention known strictly outside the changing room.
- If showers are limited or there is a queue, this is not the time to intensively condition, exfoliate or apply a face mask. Get in, shower and get out.
- Never urinate in a public shower.
- Never take photos in a changing room.

10 THINGS TO REMEMBER

1 *Don't be a gloating winner or a sore loser.*

2 *Arrive on time for team events and ready to participate.*

3 *Wear clean kit.*

4 *Obey the rules of your gym.*

5 *Don't hit on people in the gym or stare. Catch them afterwards if you really want to.*

6 *Play sport in the allocated sporting time. Chat later.*

7 *Keep to yourself in the changing room.*

8 *Regular team activities take priority on sporting grounds where there is no booking system.*

9 *Never take photos in group changing rooms.*

10 *Never hit on someone in a changing room.*

18

Miscellaneous etiquette

In this chapter you will learn how to:
- *tip*
- *listen to an MP3 player*
- *adjust your speech and body language*
- *drink in a bar*
- *study*
- *give and receive gifts and compliments*
- *behave towards the opposite sex.*

Tipping in Britain

DRINKS AT A BAR

If the bar has only bar staff and no waiting staff, tip by saying
'… and one for yourself' when placing the drinks order. The
barman will then add the price of one drink to your bill. If buying
in large rounds for a group, this should be done each time you buy
a round. In smaller groups, or on your own, it need only be done
once for the night.

If you are seated and the bar has waiting staff to take your order,
a 10–15 per cent tip should be added to the final bill if service
charge is not already included.

TOILETS

You need only tip if you use a product provided by the restroom attendant or if the attendant helps you in some way (for example, holds your hair back while you are sick or helps to clean a spilt drink from your shirt). Tip according to the help given by the attendant: if you use one of their products, £1 will suffice; if they help you clean an item of clothing, £5 is fair; if they hold your hair back while you are sick, anything less than £15 will look stingy.

COATS

If an establishment charges for its cloakroom use, tip 50p per coat to the cloakroom attendant. If the cloakroom does not charge, you should tip between £1.50 and £2 per coat.

DINING

When eating out, if the service was acceptable, tip between 10 and 15 per cent of the bill if service charge has not been included. If service charge has been included, there is no need to add more by way of a tip. The service charge is optional – if the service has been poor and the staff rude, you may refuse to pay it. If you have had exceptional service and service charge has already been added, it really is up to you whether you want to add more and if so, how much.

HAIR AND BEAUTY APPOINTMENTS

Hairdressers and beauticians should be tipped 10 per cent of the charge of the treatment, although if the hairdresser or beautician is used regularly, it is acceptable to tip in the form of a Christmas or New Year's bonus which should be between £20 and £100, depending on how regularly you use their services. This idea of a one-off annual bonus circumvents the problem of hairdressers or beauticians believing that you are tipping according to satisfaction with the treatment received if one week you forget to hand over your small change.

If the cab fare is less than £10, round up your cab fare to the nearest pound (for example, for a cab fare of £4.20, pay £5). If the cab fare is more that £10 but less than £20, round up the cab fare to the nearest £2 (for example, for a cab fare of £17.50, pay £19). If the cab fare is more than £20 but less than £30, round up the cab fare to the nearest £3 (for example, for a cab fare of £26.70, pay £29). And so on. If the cab driver helps with bags, an extra £1 should be tipped.

Insight

Tipping culture varies wildly from one country to another. Inform yourself before you visit foreign countries, as you'll need the knowledge as soon as you step foot on foreign soil. Several handy tipping guides can be found on the internet or in travel books.

Using toilets outside your own home

MEN

Upon entering a public men's restroom, if the room is empty, choose the urinal at either end of the row and furthest from the door. If you are the second person to enter the restroom, choose the urinal at the other end of the row, furthest from the first person. The third person, if there are five or more urinals, should choose the urinal in the middle of the row, the furthest point from the other two men. If the urinals are occupied such that the only available space is one which is adjacent to another person, use a stall or consider leaving and coming back at another time. If the queue is long, there are no stalls available and the need to relieve yourself is great, use whatever urinal is available, but eyes must be kept strictly straight ahead.

If you urinate in a stall or toilet, raise the toilet seat and replace it after use. This rule is particularly important when using unisex restrooms or a toilet in another person's house.

By all means go to the bathroom with friends, but don't call through the cubicle doors to talk when actually using the toilet. No one else using the restroom wants to hear your conversation. Always put used sanitary towels in the bins provided.

BOTH MEN AND WOMEN

Leave the restroom in the condition in which you found it. For example, don't leave paper towels strewn around. Always wash your hands thoroughly with soap after you use the toilet.

MP3 player etiquette

Although personal stereos and MP3 players are used by many to forget the world around them, the world does not in fact magically disappear upon the applying of headphones. The manner in which you use your MP3 player is a sign of respect to those around you, a way of showing who you are putting first – them or you.

EARPHONES

When wearing earphones, the removal of one, both or neither of your earphones says much about your respect for anyone you have contact with.

If a person of a similar age or younger merely says 'hello' or 'how are you', and clearly neither of you has any intention of taking the conversation past civilities, remove one earphone to say 'hello' back. However, if the other person is a person of authority or is older than you, remove both earphones. One earphone should also be removed in shops or coffee houses when paying. Keeping both earphones in implies that to you the other person does not exist.

If anyone tries to speak to you for more than 15 seconds, remove both earphones. If the person then joins you in whatever you were previously doing on your own, the MP3 player should be stored in a manner you would choose if you had no intention of using it for the next hour. This is also the case if the activity does not allow for any meaningful conversation (for example, being on overcrowded public transport together).

If you want to be the model of good MP3 player etiquette, wear only one earphone in public at all times in order to be more aware of your surroundings.

OTHER MP3 ETIQUETTE

At work, if you don't have your own office, MP3 players should only be used at times when you do not want or expect verbal contact with others. However, co-workers listening to MP3 players may always be interrupted at work, at which point, both earphones should always be removed.

When speaking to another person, if you are still listening to your MP3 player, do not head-bop or dance, particularly if they are telling you something of a serious nature. If you are with other people, never start listening to an MP3 player unless the other person also has one and suggests it.

Before deciding on a volume for your MP3 player, hold an earphone two feet away from your ear. If you can still hear it, turn it down. Don't shout over the volume in your ears. If you suspect you may be doing so, take both earphones out.

Festival/gig etiquette

General tips:

- *Don't pee anywhere someone else is going to have to stand.*
- *Don't jump the loo queue. When you do get to the head of the queue, loosen your belt in order to decrease the time spent within the toilet.*

- ▶ *When someone crowd surfing gets near you, grab an arm or leg and help out.*
- ▶ *After using the toilet, wash your hands with a bottle of water or antibacterial wipe if possible.*
- ▶ *Mosh with the rest or get out of the pit. Don't push against it.*

Library etiquette

General tips:

- ▶ *First and foremost, the library is a place of work. Think of it as a place of religious worship of the book and treat it accordingly. If you have no intention of working or reading, leave to reduce crowding.*
- ▶ *A library is neither a bar nor a bedroom. Chatting up the object of your desire will probably be unwelcome as they panic about their essay deadline and any display of affection between a couple will likely be met with irritation by other library users. Leave it for your breaks.*
- ▶ *Turn off the ringtone on mobiles, but also switch off the vibrate function. That buzzing noise is almost as bad as the 10-second clip of Avril Lavigne you turned off.*
- ▶ *Return sought-after books as soon as you are finished with them, and before the return date if possible. Under no circumstances keep the books longer than their due date.*
- ▶ *Libraries are places of silence. Although it may be related to work, do not speak in hushed tones to other people in the library or on your phone – it will still disturb.*
- ▶ *Most libraries do not allow food to be eaten, but if you come across a rare one that does, be considerate with your eating habits. Do not eat food with strong smells, or with loud crispy packets, and throw all rubbish away.*

Pregnant women

No matter how rotund the stomach, never ask a woman whether she is pregnant or make comments insinuating as much. Either she will volunteer the information herself or you should attain such knowledge from her friends. If you cannot validate the pregnancy by either of these methods, then the pregnancy may not yet be public knowledge or the woman may not be pregnant. If you suspect pregnancy, however, feel free to offer your seat and other such niceties, just don't say why you're doing it.

When dealing with a woman who you know is definitely pregnant, bear the following in mind:

▶ *The woman still requires personal space. There should be no touching of the pregnant belly without permission.*
▶ *Pregnant women get tired quickly. Be sympathetic and don't argue if they express a preference not to walk long distances or partake in strenuous activity.*
▶ *Pregnant women are not disabled. If they ask for help or seem as though they are struggling, help, but don't treat the pregnant woman as though she is incapable of doing anything for herself, particularly if the pregnancy is in the early stages.*
▶ *Never comment on how much a pregnant woman is eating unless you are her doctor.*
▶ *When speaking to a pregnant woman, speak to the woman, not the bump.*
▶ *Don't comment on or complain to a pregnant woman about their emotional mood swings. It is a hormonal imbalance that will pass.*

Swearing

Swearing has become so much a part of modern-day life that most people now consider it a form of expression rather than an offensive blow to their fragile and pure ears. There are still many, however, who object whole-heartedly to the use of the f-word, the s-word and most importantly the c-word.

If you belong to the former group, when meeting new people refrain from swearing until you have observed the norm for those people. Feel free to join in with as much profanity as you like, without fear of judgement, if the group seems to be doing the same, but it is advisable to hold off until you are sure. The c-word requires special caution.

If you belong to the latter group and are faced with a situation where you feel your ears are bleeding from the verbal assault lain upon them, remember that it is impolite to make a newcomer feel uncomfortable. Your bleeding ears will be nothing compared to their embarrassment should it be pointed out in public that their normal way of speaking is offensive. Provided that the swearing is not clearly being done around young children or deliberately to cause commotion and gasps of outrage, refrain from alerting the person to the offence in public. Instead, pull the person aside later and quietly explain that the 'others' tend to find that sort of language a bit difficult to deal with, referring to their age, for example, as a mitigating factor.

If in doubt or in public, don't swear. There is no one who will think less of you if you don't and many people who will be offended if you do. On top of which, if a situation does occur that requires the use of strong language, it will make far more of an impact coming from your normally sparkling clean lips. Be particularly cautious of swearing around authority figures, the elderly or pre-teens.

Language

Use the words 'please', 'thank you' and 'sorry' liberally, as well as 'good morning', 'good afternoon' and 'good evening'.

Drinking in bars

Most gatherings of post-pubescent friends in Britain tend to include an alcoholic beverage of some sort, whether it be beers in the park, a glass of wine over supper or vodka cokes in a bar. The trouble is, though, that often thoughts of etiquette are thrown down the sink with the remnants of the first bottle of beer. However, if practised continually on the less debauched occasions, it becomes habit to mind your drinking ps and qs even on occasions when you find it difficult to mind your step. Here are some general guidelines:

- *Always stand your round. If you cannot afford to do this, you can't afford to be there. Buying a round is not simply a matter of stumping up the cash, it is also a matter of effort. The round-buyer must battle with the bar queues and act as waiter.*
- *If the round-buyer will clearly struggle with the task, it is good manners for a second person to offer to help fetch the drinks from the bar.*
- *In the hubbub of a bar, it is often easy to forget that there is a queue. No one likes a queue jumper, even when there is isn't really a line. If you are accomplished in the art of gaining a barman's attention but it is clearly not your turn, point to the person beside you who has been waiting longer and insist that they are served first. The barman will serve you next (there's no need to point out the actual queue of 20 people who were all there before you, no one likes a martyr either) and the extra two minutes that it takes will have preserved your bar honour.*
- *Don't shout, whistle or gesticulate wildly at a barman to demand service. Attention-seeking gestures must be limited to a raise of the hand, not higher than shoulder-height, eye contact and perhaps a raise of the eyebrows. Money can be held in a hand clearly visible to the barstaff, but do not wave it – you are in a bar, not a strip club.*
- *It is okay to talk to strangers at the bar. It is indeed one of the only places where it is socially acceptable to do so. Make the most of it.*

- *Only order champagne if you have something to celebrate. That thing to celebrate may be minor, but it smacks of a flashy lack of taste to order a bottle of champagne loudly for no good reason.*
- *Do not force alcohol onto others or put them in a situation where peer pressure may force them to drink. Remember that it is each person's decision how inebriated they become and buying double shots for someone when they have requested a single is generous but sometimes very unwelcome, not to mention dangerous.*
- *Watch those who are driving carefully. If a designated driver has clearly had too much to drink, speak to them quietly about alternative forms of transport home or switching to soft drinks. If they become insistent that they can still drive as they are, make the others travelling with the driver aware of the situation. Find an alternative method of returning home yourself and help others unfamiliar with the area to do the same. Insist that the driver also takes an alternative form of transport. Confiscate the driver's keys if necessary. As angry as they may seem at the time, is it far better to do this than chance a dangerous journey home.*
- *These days it is acceptable to drink at any point after midday. Do it before midday and you risk looking like an alcoholic or a student. Ironically, not drinking at all looks like you are a recovering alcoholic, but if that's your choice, don't cave in to peer pressure.*

Punctuality

Be on time. Don't assume that someone else's time is less valuable than your own. If you are going to be late, warn the other person as early as possible.

Opening doors

Whoever gets to the door first opens it, male or female, and lets the other person walk through first.

Sneezing

If the urge to sneeze tickles you at a particularly bad moment, for example, during the speaking of your wedding vows, rub your tongue against the roof of your mouth to delay the sneeze until a more suitable moment.

Practise sneezing quietly. Carry tissues or a handkerchief for this eventuality, but if you cannot reach one in time, sneeze into your elbow rather than your hands to constrain the spray. If you do sneeze into your hands, wash them as soon as possible.

Body language

Be mindful that your body language may be betraying feelings that someone with good manners wouldn't express. Whole books have been written on the topic of body language, but for starters try the following:

▶ *Mind your invasion of everyone else's personal space. Don't drape yourself over a chair that someone else is sitting on. If someone takes a step back, don't automatically take a step forward.*
▶ *When trying to be welcoming and approachable, don't cross your arms.*
▶ *Don't scowl when you are asked a favour or given a task you dislike.*

Specific etiquette pointers for him and her

HIM

▶ *Walk on the traffic side of the pavement to protect women from splashes and swerving cars.*

- *Never speak to a woman's breasts. Maintain eye contact.*
- *Accompany women all the way to the door of their hotel or home if they feel unsafe, particularly at night.*
- *Hold out a lady's chair for her to be seated at a table.*
- *Don't assume that women are intellectually inferior or incompetent in day-to-day life. Help from men is nice, but not a necessity.*
- *Don't tell sexist jokes, particularly to women.*
- *Always open a lady's door to a car before letting yourself in.*
- *If a lady is in heels and you have to park some distance away from the venue to which you are travelling, offer to drop her at the venue and park the car alone.*

HER

- *If a man does you a favour, don't consider it a blow to your independence.*
- *Don't play up to being vulnerable – if you feel unsafe, say so, but don't put men or other women to extra unnecessary effort if you feel that you will survive on your own. For example, don't make a man walk you all the way to your door if you live a long way away – take a licensed cab on your own instead.*
- *If a man opens your car door first, get in and lean over to unlock his door from the inside, particularly if it is raining.*

Exam etiquette

Before the exam, rules of etiquette require that you do not admit to having studied much. Pretend to be unprepared, it will make others feel more at ease with their own panic. If it is obvious to all that you have been swotting for weeks, use an excuse, some negative comment about your studying habits which will level the score with those less prepared. Something such as, 'Yes, but I've always been terrible at this subject' or 'I spend hours at my desk but all I do is eat biscuits' normally works a treat.

After the exam, pretend you have done badly, or express neutrality at best. It is the only way to succeed socially as delight alienates those worried about their performance. Don't volunteer information on how a question should have been answered unless you harbour ambitions of social rejection and dying alone in a cave without anyone noticing or caring. Don't tell someone who looks like they are going to cry how well you think you have done, or that maybe they should have studied a little more. No, really, remember the cave and think again.

When getting your results, be aware of who has done well and who has done badly. Do not belittle the achievements of others even if you have done better. Unless someone has failed outright do not offer condolences until it is clear that the person is upset by their score, at which point, no matter how low, try to find positive words such as 'You don't need it for the job you want anyway'.

For those who have done well, success should always be attributed to luck rather than hard graft. The successful, after an initial outburst of joy, may not talk about how clever they are and should only repeatedly punch the air in isolation. However, parents should be called immediately so that they can share in the triumph.

Parents: there is no need to tell your friends and extended family more than once that your offspring has done terribly well in their exams. Limit celebratory phone calls to those who genuinely care, rather than those you want to boast to. As the fruit of your loins, it is as bad as highlighting your own success. You may be proud of what your strong genetics have provided the world, but saying so is childish and smug, particularly to those parents with less gifted children.

Students: be nice to parents at graduation. They have just put you through years of study, now is not the time to make your embarrassment of them clear.

Gift giving

Useful tips include:

- *If you are giving a gift for a special occasion, try to make sure that it gets to the person on time.*
- *If you are unsure whether an occasion calls for a gift, take or send one. If you are unsure whether the person would feel uncomfortable receiving your gift, for example, it may highlight that others have not brought gifts, take along a small wrapped gift (cufflinks or earrings) in your handbag or suit pocket that can be given in private.*
- *If it is obvious that you should provide a gift (for example, on birthdays), give the gift substantial thought. Buy something that reflects the recipient's own tastes rather than your own. The present doesn't have to be expensive to be effective if it is a personal and well thought-out gift.*
- *When giving the gift, if the contents are likely to cause embarrassment (for example, if you have bought lingerie), insist that the recipient opens the present in private.*
- *Don't leave the price tag on.*
- *Put some effort into the wrapping to make it decorative.*
- *Give gifts whenever you can. Some of the most appreciated ones are those given for no reason at all other than friendship or love.*

Gift receiving

If possible, try to open the gift immediately. The pleasure for the giver will be in seeing your reaction. Always show enthusiasm for the gift. Never ask for the receipt to swap it for something else. If you are opening presents from several people with an audience, try to show similar levels of emotion and gratitude for all the gifts received. If you felt that more thought or effort was put in by some givers, find them later to express particular gratitude.

Don't hand on presents to others as presents.

> **Insight**
> Always say 'thank you' and express extreme delight when receiving a gift. Any gift, however small, will have taken time to source and wrap.

Theatres and live shows

Turn your mobile phone and BlackBerry off. If seating is not pre-allocated, never try to reserve more than two seats for people not yet present.

Guessing ages

For those over 25, minus five years from whatever you think is the true age.

For those between 20 and 25, minus one year.

For teenagers, add two years.

For pre-teens, try to get the age exactly right.

How to accept a compliment

Say 'thank you' and return with a compliment equally as generous and genuine immediately or later on if one does not come naturally.

Children

General tips include:

- *If you have small children, it is your duty as a parent to keep them from being a nuisance to others. It is not the job of anyone else to entertain them. If a kindly person has taken on this task, bear in mind that after 15 minutes they should be relieved unless you are paying them (for example, babysitters).*
- *Teach your children to have good table manners, how to have a polite conversation and impress on them the importance of keeping quiet when necessary. Behave with good manners yourself and your child will grow to mimic you.*
- *Afford your children the same respect that you would like to receive from them. Don't cut them off mid-sentence to say something yourself, for example, and where possible, respect their privacy and choice of friends. Say 'please', 'thank you' and 'sorry' where necessary.*
- *Share duties with other parents, making sure that you offer as many favours regarding your children as you receive.*
- *Never assume that your children are invited to events. If their names aren't on the invitation, hire a babysitter rather than putting your host in the awkward position of having to explain why they would prefer not to have children present.*
- *As a host, if you want to hold an event without particular children of your friends, you must make the event a widespread 'no children' affair.*
- *Bear in mind that your friends, particularly those without children, are unlikely to want to hear details of your child's day-to-day life and achievements. Children will naturally be a big part of your life but if you are telling a story about them, try to keep it as brief as possible and try to keep it humorous or genuinely interesting.*

Family and friends

It becomes easy to take the people closest to you for granted as you slip into familiar routines. However, consider regularly whether the routine to which you have become accustomed is a fair distribution of duties. In addition, make sure that the onus of paying does not always fall to the same person and that the effort of visiting each other is always shared, even if one of you lives in a nicer or more vibrant place. Make sure you both make the effort to call each other. If you feel that one of your friends or family always makes more effort than you do, up your game.

No matter how close you are to your friends and family, always remember that their home is part of their personal space. Give some warning before you land yourself on their doorstep to check that your visit will not inconvenience them and although the phrase 'make yourself at home' may be bandied about with abandon, never do. For example, ask before you take items from the fridge, borrow books or change the radio station or TV channel. If you do, with your friend or family's permission, borrow an item from their home, return it as soon as you are finished with it in the condition you borrowed it. Never borrow an item for longer than a month unless you have gained a friend or family member's explicit permission to do so.

10 THINGS TO REMEMBER

1 *If in doubt about whether to tip, tip.*

2 *Leave bathrooms the way you found them.*

3 *When people try to have a conversation with you, remove the earphones of your music player.*

4 *Don't jump queues.*

5 *Respect the personal space of pregnant women but also offer help where possible.*

6 *Don't swear in public.*

7 *Use the words 'please', 'thank you' and 'sorry' liberally.*

8 *Always stand your round in bars.*

9 *Be on time.*

10 *Give compliments generously and receive them modestly.*

Conclusion

The contents of this book are not intended to be taken as a rigorous list determining polite behaviour in this day and age. From day to day and from situation to situation, the 'right' thing to do may take an unexpected spin on what has been written here. Being a kind person with honourable intentions will always be more important than knowing which knife and fork to use at supper, but a knowledge of accepted modern manners and etiquette is a sign of respect to those around you.

Observe the ebb, flow, hustle, bustle, confusion and chaos of everyday life and do your best to not attack the sensibilities of friends, family, work colleagues and complete strangers. Embrace etiquette today as a sign of goodness rather than money or class – consider what you have read here simply a starting point to a more considerate you.

Taking it further

Most of the chapters of this book, and in some cases, even sub-chapters, have had great tomes devoted to the specific etiquette of the situation. Although modern manners is a fluid concept, for some more detailed guidelines, you may like to leaf through the pages of the following books.

Debrett's Correct Form, (Debrett's Ltd, 2006).

Titles and Forms of Address: A Guide to Correct Use (A & C Black Publishers Ltd, 2007)

Blackstone-Ford, J., Jupe, S. *Ex-Etiquette for Holidays and Other Family Celebrations* (Chicago Review Press, 2007).

Campbell, D. *The Bride Wore Black Leather ... and He Looked Fabulous: An Etiquette Guide for the Rest of Us* (Greenery Press, US, 2001).

Carlson, R. *The Don't Sweat Guide to Entertaining: Enjoying Friends More While Worrying Less* (Hyperion, 2004).

Charles, M. *Debrett's Guide to Entertaining: The Complete Guide of Modern Entertaining* (Headline Book Publishing, 1994).

Clayton, N. *A Butler's Guide to Table Manners* (National Trust Books, 2007).

Dallas, J. *When Homosexuality Hits Home: What to Do When a Loved One Says They're Gay* (Harvest House Publishers, 2004).

Devereux, G.R.M. *Etiquette for Men: A Book of Modern Manners and Customs* (Bounty Books, 2002).

Dresser, N. *Multicultural Celebrations: Today's Rules of Etiquette for Life's Special Occasions* (Three Rivers Pr, 1999).

Fodor *All About Tipping* (Fodor's Travel Publications Inc, 2002).

Glazier *What Never to Say to Pregnant Women: A Guide to Pregnancy Etiquette* (Spectacle Lane Press, Inc, 1996).

Kallos, J. *Because Netiquette Matters!* (Xlibris Corporation, 2004).

Kavet, G., Robin, A. *Saving Face: How to Lie, Fake and Manoeuvre Your Way Out of Life's Most Awkward Situations* (Simon & Schuster Childrens Books, 2005).

Lenius, O. *A Well-dressed Gentleman's Pocket Guide* (Prion Books Ltd, 2006).

Lucas, S. *The Art of Public Speaking* (McGraw-Hill Education, 2000).

Maggio, R. *The Art of Talking to Anyone: Essential People Skills for Success in Any Situation* (McGraw-Hill Higher Education, 2007).

Matlins *Perfect Stranger's Guide to Funerals and Grieving* (SkyLight Paths Publishing, US, 2000).

Mills, Y. *How to Party: Everything You Need to Know About Throwing a Successful Party* (Rooftop Publishing, 2006).

Mole, J. *Mind Your Manners: Managing Business Culture in a Global Europe* (Nicholas Brealey Publishing Ltd, 2003).

Naylor, S. *The Essential Guide to Wedding Etiquette* (Sourcebooks, Inc, 2006).

Powell, P. *Behave Yourself! The Essential Guide to International Etiquette* (Insiders' Guide, 2005).

Repenski, K. *The Complete Idiot's Guide to Successful Dressing* (Alpha Books, 1998).

Roane, S. *How to Work a Room, Fully Revised and Updated: The Ultimate Guide to Savvy Socializing In-Person and On-Line* (Robson Books Ltd, 2002).

Sinclair, K. *Mobile Mayhem: Life, Mobile Phones and All That* (Take That, 1999).

Strawbridge, M. *Netiquette: Internet Etiquette in the Age of the Blog* (Software Reference Ltd, 2006).

Taylor, L.C., Burgess, V., Robb, D. *The Etiquette of Dating* (Gibbs M. Smith Inc, 2003).

Taylor, L.C., Burgess, V., Robb, D. *The Etiquette of Parenting* (Gibbs M. Smith Inc, 2003).

Wainwright, G.R. *Teach Yourself Body Language* (Hodder Education, 2003).

West, K. *How to Raise a Gentleman: A Civilized Guide to Helping Your Son Through His Uncivilized Childhood* (Rutledge Hill Press, US, 2003).

Whitmore, J. *Business Class: Etiquette Essentials for Success at Work* (St. Martin's Press, 2005).

Index